Personal Productivity
Tips and Tools for Daily Success

Development Dimensions International, Inc.

© MCMXCVII by Development Dimensions International, Inc.

Published by DDI Press, c/o Development Dimensions International, World Headquarters—Pittsburgh, 1225 Washington Pike, Bridgeville, Pennsylvania 15017–2838.

Manufactured in the United States of America.

Library of Congress Cataloging-in-Publications Data:

Development Dimensions International, Inc.
Personal Productivity: Tips and Tools for Daily Success

1. Business
2. Self-Help

ISBN 0-9623483-8-4

10 9 8 7 6 5 4 3 2 1

Personal Productivity: Tips and Tools for Daily Success

How to Use This Book

Are you tired of juggling too many top priorities? Are you endlessly interrupted? Are you confused because you don't know where to go or who to turn to when you need information or support? Or maybe you're a chronic procrastinator. You'll worry about that later, right? If you answered "yes" to any of these questions, don't feel too bad—you're not alone.

In today's fast-paced world, almost everyone constantly faces new information, increased responsibilities, and rapidly changing technology. Successful people are able to sort through and adapt to it all, while maintaining high levels of performance. How do they do it? Simple: They use the tips and tools for daily success contained in this book. The good news is that you can too!

This book was designed for the "terminally busy," the kind of people who need to achieve good business results quickly and effectively. It won't bog you down with a lot of theory or background information. Rather, the pages are filled with easy-to-use tips and tools to boost your personal productivity quickly.

What This Means to You

Did you ever think you can't change or improve the way things are done in your organization, department, or work group? Well, think again. This book contains 18 topics aimed at helping you improve your personal effectiveness. No matter where you work or what your job is, these tips and tools will make a difference, with one key ingredient—your commitment.

How to Find What You Need

Think of this book as a survival guide. As you face new and challenging situations or encounter productivity problems, turn to the appropriate pages in the book for just-in-time help. How you find the help you need is up to you. Depending on how you prefer to learn, you can take any of three approaches to determine which topics you should read about first.

Three Approaches

1. **Table of Contents.** If you feel most comfortable with a structured approach, turn to the Table of Contents on page 1 and select a topic that interests you.
2. **Illustrated Map.** More visually oriented readers might appreciate the illustrated map on pages 2–3. When you see a topic that interests you, just go to the appropriate page and get started.
3. **Where to Begin? (Quiz).** If you're not quite sure where to start or what you need help with, take a few minutes to complete the Where to Begin? quiz on page 7. It will help you identify areas for improvement and direct you to those pages.

Then, There Are Icons!

Illustrations and icons are used throughout this book to identify features such as links to related topics or helpful hints to increase your chances of success. Here are the icons you will encounter on your productivity journey.

Link to . . .

When you see this segment of chain, look for links to other topics in the book. Corresponding page numbers are included to help you make the connection.

Helpful Hint

These productivity boosters will really give you a lift when you read the helpful hints they provide.

Caution

Look before you leap! This icon identifies common productivity mistakes and barriers and indicates what you can do to avoid them.

You Try It!

As you navigate your way through the book, you'll encounter a few "notable" opportunities to practice and give these tools a try. Pull out a pen and make your mark!

Additional Tools and Tactics

Don't Slip Back

This topic can ensure that you maintain your momentum by helping you anticipate and avoid productivity pitfalls. You'll keep your commitment to be more productive by using the Pitfall Planner to record the new approaches you plan to take and how you'll stick with them.

Personal Productivity Group Discussion Guide

While you can significantly boost your productivity by experimenting on your own with the tips, tools, and tactics in this book, you can also help others who are experiencing similar situations or challenges. The discussion questions in this last section of the book are intended to help you and your coworkers, team members, and internal partners tackle tough productivity issues together.

Where to Begin?

If you're not sure which topic you should begin working on, take the following quick quiz. Answer each question by checking either YES or NO. If you check any NO's in a particular topic, turn to that topic in the book for information that will help you to be more productive. The more NO answers you have in a category, the more you need to tackle that topic.

Examining Your Priorities (page 14)

YES	NO	
☐	☐	1. Do you spend time on activities that support the organization's vision and goals?
☐	☐	2. Do you know what's important to your customers?
☐	☐	3. Are you able to avoid spending a lot of time putting out fires and reacting to important and urgent problems?
☐	☐	4. Do you know what kinds of activities help prevent crises and build competence?

What to Do When Everything Is Top Priority (page 18)

YES	NO	
☐	☐	1. Are you aware of the five most common Priority Pitfalls?
☐	☐	2. Do you know how to avoid Priority Pitfalls?
☐	☐	3. Do you know a smart way to handle urgent requests?
☐	☐	4. Do you feel comfortable saying "no" to others when appropriate?
☐	☐	5. Do you know what to do if you can't meet a goal that you agreed to?

Staying on Track (page 22)

YES	NO	
☐	☐	1. Do you know how to avoid detours from your priorities at work and to stay on track?
☐	☐	2. Can you recognize the signs that tell you whether you're on or off the right track?
☐	☐	3. Do you know what to do if you get off track?

Organizing Your Work Area (page 25)

YES	NO	
☐	☐	1. Can you find the material or information you need in a minute or less?
☐	☐	2. Do you know the number one technique for getting organized?
☐	☐	3. Are your work area and files well organized?
☐	☐	4. Do you know how to stay organized once you get organized?

Keeping Track of Your Time and Tasks (page 28)

YES	NO	
☐	☐	1. Are you on time and prepared for every meeting you attend?
☐	☐	2. Do you remember and keep all your commitments?
☐	☐	3. Do you know the best scheduling tool to use for your job?
☐	☐	4. Do you know the top five ways to ensure that you're getting the most from your calendar or planner?

Handling Interruptions (page 31)

YES	NO	
☐	☐	1. Can you tell the difference between necessary and unnecessary interruptions?
☐	☐	2. Do you know what to do when visitors wear out their welcome?
☐	☐	3. Do you know how to prevent interruptions?
☐	☐	4. Do you know how to keep interruptions to a minimum?

Making Meetings Productive (page 34)

YES	NO	
☐	☐	1. Do you know when a meeting is—and is not—the most appropriate way to address a situation?
☐	☐	2. Do you know the seven best practices for organizing a productive meeting?
☐	☐	3. Do you know how to deal with common disruptive meeting behaviors?
☐	☐	4. Do you use a checklist to ensure that you have everything you need for a successful meeting?

Making a Basic Plan (page 39)

YES	NO	
☐	☐	1. Do you know when it's essential to have a plan?
☐	☐	2. Do you know the six best questions to ask when making a plan?
☐	☐	3. Do you have a plan for keeping track of ongoing projects?
☐	☐	4. Do you know when to make contingency plans?

Making the Best Use of Communication Tools (page 45)

YES	NO	
☐	☐	1. Do you know when it's best to use voice mail?
☐	☐	2. Do you know when it's inappropriate to use e-mail?
☐	☐	3. Do you know how to get quick responses to your messages when needed?
☐	☐	4. Do you know the six things your voice mail message should include?
☐	☐	5. Do you know when a live conversation is better than voice mail?
☐	☐	6. Do you know when it's best to put your message in writing?

Networking (page 49)

YES	NO	
☐	☐	1. Do you know what "networking" means?
☐	☐	2. Do you know who to go to when you need information outside of your department?
☐	☐	3. Are you part of an information- and idea-sharing network on your job?
☐	☐	4. Do you know how to make contact with your network partners?
☐	☐	5. Do you know how to make your network work for you?

Getting Support from Others (page 53)

YES	NO	
☐	☐	1. Do you know when to ask for support?
☐	☐	2. Do you know who to ask for support?
☐	☐	3. Do you know the right way to ask for support?
☐	☐	4. Do you know how to acknowledge the support you receive?

Making Clear Agreements (page 58)

YES	NO	
☐	☐	1. Do you know what causes unclear agreements?
☐	☐	2. Do you know the top five strategies for making clear agreements?
☐	☐	3. Can you create a good role clarity chart?
☐	☐	4. Do you know what to do if someone is unhappy with an agreement?
☐	☐	5. Do you know how to proactively ensure that all your future agreements will be clear?

Being a Good Partner (page 64)

YES	NO	
☐	☐	1. Do you know if you are being a good partner at work?
☐	☐	2. Do you know the five best ways to be a good partner?
☐	☐	3. Can you list the most common ways that people damage partnerships?
☐	☐	4. Do you know how to build better partnerships?
☐	☐	5. Do you know how to measure the success of your partnerships?

Effective Follow-Up (page 68)

YES	NO	
☐	☐	1. Do you work entirely alone, without any help from others?
☐	☐	2. Do you know how to "let go" while "staying close"?
☐	☐	3. Do you know the "do's and don'ts" of following up?
☐	☐	4. Do you have an effective tool to ensure that others keep their work commitments to you?

Keeping Yourself Motivated in Tough Times (page 73)

YES	NO	
☐	☐	1. Have you developed a coping technique for difficult situations?
☐	☐	2. Do you know the benefits of changing your attitude?
☐	☐	3. Can you turn a demotivating situation into a motivating one?
☐	☐	4. Do you know how to reward yourself for a job well done?

Recognizing and Avoiding Perfectionism (page 79)

YES	NO	
☐	☐	1. Do you know that perfectionism is not a good thing?
☐	☐	2. Do you know the difference between doing a great job and perfectionism?
☐	☐	3. Do you know when "good enough" is good enough?
☐	☐	4. Do you know the best ways to ensure quality performance without being a perfectionist?

Conquering Procrastination (page 85)

YES	NO	
☐	☐	1. Are your jobs always completed on schedule or ahead of time?
☐	☐	2. Do you do things today if you know they can wait until tomorrow?
☐	☐	3. Do you greet challenging new jobs by jumping right in and getting started?
☐	☐	4. Are you aware of the effect of your procrastination on your coworkers?
☐	☐	5. Do you know the number one tool to eliminate procrastination?

Don't Slip Back (page 91) (This section will be most helpful after you have completed some of the other topics.)

YES	NO	
☐	☐	1. Once you've made a behavior change, do you use the improved behavior regularly?
☐	☐	2. Do you know when the temptation to slip back into unproductive behavior is the strongest?
☐	☐	3. Do you have a strategy in place to avoid returning to nonproductive behavior?

Examining Your Priorities

Have you ever gotten so caught up in doing something "right" that you didn't stop to think about whether it was the "right thing to do"? Have you been doing your job the same way for so long that you just assume you're focusing on the highest priorities? Has an internal customer ever complained that your group is more focused on following its own processes than on meeting the needs of customers?

If you answered yes to any of these questions, you need to examine your priorities and evaluate how you spend your time. For your long-term career success, it's critical to focus your time and energy on the kinds of activities that will:

- Contribute to your customers' success and satisfaction.
- Support the organization's strategic vision and goals.
- Boost your personal productivity and performance.

Finding Out What's Important

Assessing your priorities to ensure that they meet the three criteria above requires a little detective work—especially in times of change. Here's a sampling of sources you can tap into.

- **Your customers.** They're the reason your business is in business! Satisfying your customers means understanding what's important to them and fulfilling their needs and wants.

- **Your boss.** Discover what's important to your department or division by hearing it straight from the horse's mouth.

- **Your boss' boss.** Looking at the forest from the tops of the trees can give you a whole new perspective and appreciation for what you need to do and why.

- **Your most successful coworkers.** The people doing the job well know it best! Seek star performers and follow their leads by asking questions, observing their behavior, and applying what you learn.

- **Your organization's vision, values, mission, or business plans.** These should be sources of direction and purpose for anyone in the organization.

- **Your performance plan.** Many organizations use performance plans as a way to clearly communicate and implement organizational strategies, as well as focus on individual growth and development. Consult your plan and uncover your priorities.

When finding out what's important, be sure to ask others who have jobs and experiences different from yours. These people can shine a different light on your role. Choose a good cross section of people throughout the organization to give you the broadest perspective possible.

Easy Interview Guide

If you've ever dreamed of becoming a daytime talk show host, here's your chance! After you decide *who* to interview, you need to decide *what* you're going to ask. Maximize your interview time by creating and following a prepared interview guide. Here are a few key questions you might ask to broaden your perspective and help you learn what's important to your organization, customers, internal partners, manager, and coworkers.

1. What are the organization's/department's strategic goals and objectives?

2. How does my work help the organization achieve these goals and objectives?

3. What are your expectations for my work/project/product?

4. What would you like to see me start doing, stop doing, or continue doing?

5. What skills and behaviors should I demonstrate in order to be perceived as highly valuable to the organization?

After you have a clear understanding of what's important, you need to make sure you are focusing your time and energy on doing "the right things" and on doing them right.

Getting Your Priorities Straight with the Urgency/Importance Grid

All priorities are not created equal. And, when you've got multiple customers and multiple projects, it can be extremely challenging to determine how best to use your valuable time. This grid provides a simple way to assess your priorities and decide how to divide your time in order to accomplish them.

	Urgent	Not Urgent
Important	(A) Do It Now	(B) Do It Soon
Not Important	(C) Do I Really Need to Do This?	(D) Don't Do It!

(A) Do It Now (Urgent & Important). These assignments typically top your list. They are time-critical activities that contribute to the achievement of your goals. Time spent on these activities is reactive and focused on solving immediate problems. Here are some examples of (A) priorities:

- Project deadlines
- Medical emergencies
- Customer complaints and requests

(B) Do It Soon (Not Urgent & Important). These are the things that proactively contribute to goal achievement but are not time critical. Often overlooked but very important, these activities help prevent crises and build competence to handle emergencies more efficiently when they do arise. These would be (B) priorities:

- Planning projects or assignments
- Preparing for future events
- Networking

(C) Do I Really Need to Do This? (Urgent & Not Important). These tasks are reactive, time-critical assignments that do not contribute to goal achievement. Ask yourself, *"Do I really need to do this now?"* If the task doesn't contribute to an important goal, it might be a waste of time. Following are some examples of (C) priorities:

- Routine interruptions
- Some reports
- Some phone calls

(D) Don't Do It! (Not Urgent & Not Important). These assignments are not time critical and do not contribute to important objectives. Ask yourself, *"Do these assignments reflect organizational, departmental, or customer-oriented priorities? Or, am I doing these activities to avoid working on what's really important?"* Consider the consequences of ignoring these activities and factor that into your decision. Avoid the following:

- Junk mail
- Socializing
- Trivia
- Procrastination
- Busywork
- Some phone calls

You Try It!

Take a sheet of blank paper and jot down all the things that you need to accomplish today or this week. When you are finished, consider the urgency and importance of each task and label it A, B, C, or D. To boost your personal productivity and performance, start working on those priorities that you labeled **(A) Do It Now** and **(B) Do It Soon.**

Link to . . .

You'll find further assistance on related subjects in the following sections: *What to Do When Everything Is Top Priority* on page 18 and *Networking* on page 49.

What to Do When Everything Is Top Priority

Ever Get the Feeling . . .

You're juggling too many balls (or chainsaws in this case!) in the air? You have too many high-priority responsibilities and too little time. With so many urgent tasks, you have trouble doing any of them well.

Priority Pitfalls

Sometimes having too much to do isn't the real problem. Often, you unintentionally make your job harder than it needs to be by falling into a Priority Pitfall. Which of the following have you done?

- ☐ Oversimplified your tasks and underestimated the amount of time it would take to complete them. Have you ever spread yourself too thin?

- ☐ Made things harder than they needed to be. Have you ever involved 20 people in making a small, relatively insignificant decision?

- ☐ Handled work inefficiently. Have you ever received feedback that you could accomplish more in less time or complete certain tasks more quickly?

- ☐ Underutilized resources and support. How often have you turned down help when it was offered because you thought you could do it better and faster on your own?

- ☐ Allowed too many "false priorities" to slip onto your plate. Have you ever accepted additional tasks or responsibilities without checking how urgent they really were?

List some personal pitfalls you've encountered:

....

....

....

....

Tips for Avoiding Priority Pitfalls

- **Negotiate deadlines.** You might be surprised to find that some of your priorities really aren't priorities at all! Ask questions like *"How urgent is this?" "What do you mean when you say, 'as soon as possible'?"* or *"Would tomorrow be all right?"* They'll help you avoid working on false priorities.

- **Sequence your tasks for greatest efficiency.** When dealing with complex assignments, you can gain a productivity advantage by sequencing your tasks for greatest efficiency.

Helpful Hint

Begin by outlining all your tasks (including any smaller pieces of those tasks). Then, put them in a logical order. For example, find out everything you need to know about a new assignment, including what resources you'll need, before you begin so you won't need to interrupt your momentum to change direction or waste time waiting on a resource.

- **Stockpile work or questions.** Another way to eliminate inefficiency is to "stockpile" similar tasks. For example, rather than running to the photocopy machine every time you need to make a copy, wait until you have several things that need to be copied and do them all in one trip. Or, if you need to ask your boss a minor question or have a brief discussion, keep a note of it until you have several items. Then you can handle them all in one conversation instead of several.

- **Do a reality check.** When someone asks you for help, ask questions to determine exactly what needs to be done by when. This will help you set realistic goals for accomplishing your assignments and minimize priority pileup.

- **Show your cards.** Let people who need your help know that you have several priorities. When they are aware of your priorities, they might be the first to suggest that theirs is not really urgent.

- **Seek support.** If you are responsible for tasks that others are willing—and able—to handle, ask for help.

- **Just say no.** You won't do any favors by saying yes to a job that you know you can't possibly accomplish on time. If you have the option to tell someone that you can't take on a particular assignment, try to offer a few alternatives. For example, you might say:
  - *"I could fit this in next week if it can wait until then."*
  - *"If we can find someone to take over the assignment I'm working on right now, then I could take on this one."*
  - *"If you can give me a few days' notice next time, I'll be able to plan ahead and help you."*

  Saying no too often won't win friends or respect. Decline to help others only if offering your time would truly jeopardize your higher-priority tasks. Remember that saying yes to a request for help is a great way to build partnerships with others and boost customer satisfaction.

- **Go the extra mile (when you can).** Yes, you do have a life outside of work. Nobody expects you to work around the clock to keep up with your work priorities. That said, sometimes putting in extra time every now and then can keep you from getting overloaded and falling behind. Peace of mind and the appreciation of your coworkers can be well worth the time.

What to Do if You Can't Meet an Agreed-Upon Goal or Date

One of the quickest ways to erode trust is by missing a goal that you agreed to—especially if it happens on a regular basis! Sometimes, however, no matter what you do, you're going to miss a deadline. It happens to the best of us. So what should you do when you can't meet a commitment? Minimize the impact on your working relationships by following some basic do's and don'ts.

DO	DON'T
■ Warn people who expect work from you that you might not complete it on time.	■ Let the deadline come and go without any warning, notification, or follow-up.
■ Ask the person for help in trying to avoid a potential delay.	■ Make excuses for missing the deadline.
■ Initiate a contingency plan, such as seeking resources/support to help you accomplish your tasks by or near your negotiated deadline.	■ Dump it back on the person without warning or offering to explore other ways of getting the job done.
■ Admit that you've made a planning mistake and need some help to correct it.	■ Point fingers or blame others for a slip in the schedule that they didn't cause or couldn't prevent.
■ If possible, renegotiate deadlines to get an extension.	■ Procrastinate and push back the date until you are ready to do the job.
■ Explain what you'll do next time to avoid missing agreed-upon goals.	■ Avoid taking on future assignments and lending a helping hand.

For additional information, see *Examining Your Priorities* on page 14.

Link to . . .

Staying on Track

Staying focused on the kinds of activities that your organization, customers, and coworkers consider important can be a tough task.

You need to keep your eyes on the road ahead and your attention on the task at hand. Listen to the traffic reports and beware of detours (as well as signs of success) as you move forward.

Tips for Avoiding Detours

One way to be sure you stay on the right track is not to get off it in the first place! Here are a few tips to help you avoid potential detours and keep you on course.

- **Post your priorities.** Once you've gotten your priorities straight, try to keep them that way by posting them in a prominent place where you can see them at all times. This continual reminder of what's important can help keep you from veering off the track.

- **Monitor your progress.** Mark milestones by checking off items as you complete them. Not only will this ensure that you're staying on track, it will also give you a personal boost from a feeling of accomplishment as you make progress.

- **Seek feedback.** Keep your eyes and ears open for signs to confirm your direction. Feedback from others on your performance can help you steer away from trouble by pointing out potential roadblocks as well as areas for improvement. With that information, you can make adjustments to keep you (or even get you back) on track.

Even when you've taken these precautions, sometimes you still might find that you're spending time doing the wrong things. Here are some telltale signs to help you recognize when you're on the right track or when you've strayed from the course.

You're on the Right Track When . . .

- Your customers, boss, and peers appreciate your efforts and praise your accomplishments.
- You receive high ratings on your performance appraisal.
- You very rarely experience crises on the job that could have been avoided.
- You're often considered for additional responsibility, special projects, and the "best," most challenging assignments.
- You can easily explain how your work positively contributes to the organization's success.
- You feel good about your work and are energized by it.
- Your hard work and efforts pay off in the results.

You Know You're Off Course When . . .

- You're working really hard, but you're not really getting anything done.
- You receive low ratings on your performance plan.
- Your customers call to complain.
- You are the only one who seems to think that you're doing a great job.
- You're not really sure why you're doing what you're doing or when it needs to be done.
- You're always putting out fires—yours and others.
- You spend a lot of time socializing or complaining.
- You're not sure what's important to the organization or what your priorities are.

What to Do If You Derail

Staying on track is not an easy task; it takes a lot of work and dedication. In the event that you do get sidetracked, here are a few things you can do to get back on course quickly.

- **Shake your compass.** If you know you're missing the mark, stop and look at your priorities again. Realign your goals and assignments, if necessary, before moving ahead. Don't wait too long before you decide to turn around; the sooner you correct yourself, the better!

- **Ask for directions.** Sometimes you're just not sure when, where, or even how you got off track. Ask people with whom you work very closely for help in determining these factors. Then seek their guidance and advice about how best to get back on track based on their knowledge and experiences.

- **Raise a "red flag."** If you've realized that you need to correct your course, let others know about it. Coworkers or your leader can confirm the best course with you. Also, if you know you've made a misstep, chances are someone else has noticed too. By sharing how you'll correct your course, you'll rebuild others' confidence in you.

Write down a few of your own ideas to get back on track:

....

....

....

....

....

Organizing Your Work Area

☐ Do you have stacks of unorganized stuff on your work surface or desk?

☐ If you need to find something in your work area, can you find it in 10 seconds? 10 minutes? 10 hours?

☐ Has your work space been zoned for archeological digs?

If you felt a little uncomfortable as you read this list, you probably need the Home Base technique. If you can imagine your coworkers thinking of you—and chuckling—as they read this list, you *definitely* need it. One of the most common ways that people undermine their own productivity is by failing to organize the materials, tools, and information needed to do their jobs.

The Number One Way to Get Organized

Create a Home Base
Create a home—a location, file, spot, or place—for everything you need to get your job done.

You don't have to have a completely object-free work area to be well organized, but you do need one that doesn't embarrass you, hinder your productivity, make you crazy, or make others think that you're not on top of the job.

So, if you have trouble finding things on your work surface, try a combination of the following tips for creating a home base.

■ **Get rid of the major clutter.** If you use something often but not constantly, create a home base for it that's *not* on your work surface. Don't just stuff it into the nearest drawer. Take a few minutes to think about where it would be most convenient for you.

■ **Stash it creatively.** Can you mount it on the wall? Can you hang it from the back of your chair? Will an inexpensive shelf do the trick?

- **Decide on the home base by handiness, not tradition.** One computer operator kept her mouse on the left side of her keyboard for years only because that's where she found it when she replaced the former operator—who was left-handed.

- **Put it in the same place every time.** Since you've given some thought to the best place to stash something, respect your decision by putting it there *every* time you're finished with it.

- **File it.** If you use it infrequently, file it. This can be scary for people who usually stack piles of papers on any flat surface or put clumps of stuff in a file drawer. Use the tips below to make it easier for you to find what you've filed.
  - Use colors. Get some of the colorful new hanging files and folders. Or create your own color-coding system using magic markers or stickers to jazz up plain manila folders.
  - Use the ABCs. If you've been filing by your own intuitive system (and it's not working well), give the simple alphabetical or numerical systems a chance. It works pretty well for dictionaries and libraries. Alphabetical filing also gives someone else a chance to find material if they need to.

- **Color-code it.** Colors work great for keeping track of equipment and supplies. If you share a work space or just have a lot of stuff to keep track of, try a color-coding system (using tape, stickers, or paint) to make it easy to find (and return) items to the same place every time.

If You *Might* Need It, Box It

If you haven't used something in months, but you're not quite sure that you won't need it again:

1. Put the material in a box, date it, and put the box out of sight.
2. Put a reminder on your calendar to check the box in several months to see what you've been saving.
3. When that date arrives, actually check the box and get rid of things you haven't used.

What to Do with New Materials

Once you've organized the materials that are usually on your work surface, what should you do with new things that come your way?

Instead of letting new piles build up, handle incoming things just once. Handle them as soon as they come in or set aside time once or twice a day—whichever works best for you. With each item, do one of the following.

- **Trash it.** If it's junk mail, memos that don't apply to you, etc., trash it right away. Dumping the nonessentials is a great feeling!

  Thing I'll put in the trash after reading:

  ....

  ....

- **Act on it.** If it requires an action from you—call someone, sign this, return that—do it immediately. Now it's done and it won't get lost in the cracks!

  Types of materials I'll act on immediately:

  ....

  ....

- **File it.** If it must be kept, keep it where you'll be able to find it again. Use your new filing system and keep your work surface bright and clutter free!

  Files that I'll create (or update) are:

  ....

  ....

A quick tip for staying organized is to spend a few minutes at the end of each day putting everything back in its home. You'll feel good when you walk into a neat work space every day.

Keeping Track of Your Time and Tasks

☐ Are you often late for meetings or appointments?

☐ Do you sometimes find that you've double-booked an appointment time?

☐ Do you ever show up in the wrong room for a meeting?

☐ Have your coworkers or leaders needed to reschedule a meeting or visit with you because you forgot they were coming?

If you checked even two of these, you need to consider one of the following tools to get—and stay—on schedule. Today, no one has time to be amused by an absent-minded–professor type.

Which Scheduling Tools Should You Use?

To-Do Lists

If some parts of your job change from day to day, or if you occasionally have to do something out of the ordinary, a to-do list is perfect for you. It keeps things from falling through the cracks of a busy day, and there's a satisfaction in crossing off tasks as you do them.

It doesn't have to be fancy—just a little list to get your brain into gear at the beginning of the day, to help you keep track of things no matter how busy you get, and to show your progress at the end of the day. Here are some types of to-do lists.

- **Ongoing list.** Keep a small notebook by the phone or take it to meetings. In it you simply record the job you need to do, and then scratch it out when you complete it.

- **White board.** Same principle as the notebook; it's just more public (and less portable). Write jobs you need to keep track of on the board. Wipe them away as they're completed.

- **Bulletin board or "sticky notes" chart.** These let you prioritize as well as list your jobs. Because you can quickly rearrange the items on your list, you can easily redefine your to-do's and keep track of changes to the schedule.

Tracking Grid

If a lot of items must be done in sequence or come and go during the course of a few days (orders to be checked, documents that require several signatures, etc.), a tracking grid could be perfect for you. Draw a grid either by hand or on the computer; then, list in the left column the items you're tracking and enter the destinations across the top row. This is an excellent way to keep track of things. It's also a quick reference when you get a frantic phone call asking where something is. Here's an example of one used by a medical secretary.

Blood Tests for:	To Lab	From Lab	To Doctor	From Doctor	Copy to Patient	Patient Reply
Jessica Dean	2/17	2/19	2/19	2/20	2/21	2/26
Jim Byron	2/19	2/21	2/22			

Best Practices for Using a Calendar or Planner

Your schedule determines the kind of a calendar or planner you need. If you have a few things to do, or places to be, at a particular time several times a week, you're probably already using a desk or wall calendar. If you often have lots to do and places to be, you need a planner that breaks your day into hours (or quarter hours) and has built-in space for notes, reminders, and phone and fax lists. Whichever tool you use, here are tips to help you make the best use of it.

- **Don't use a calendar/planner to record only future meetings.** Use it to record all information about how you spend your time, including meetings, phone calls, and your to-do list.

- **Use your calendar/planner to record *all* your plans**—business and personal. Don't use separate papers or books to keep track of different projects. If you keep your information in only one place:
  - You'll never double-book a meeting.
  - You'll never miss an important meeting because you looked on the wrong calendar.
  - You won't waste time moving things from calendar to planner and run the risk of skipping or deleting something.

- **Look ahead to the rest of your week or month.** Hold time in your calendar to accomplish important tasks such as *"Prepare for 2:00 meeting," "Work on my performance plan,"* or *"Finish monthly report."*

- **When noting meetings in your calendar, make sure to record:**
  - What the meeting is about.
  - Where it is.
  - The key things you'll need to do or say in the meeting.

- **Always determine specific times for an activity and write it in the calendar** when making plans with others. Don't say, *"Stop by and see me sometime tomorrow"* or *"I'll give you a call later in the week."* Pick a date and a precise time for any activity or meeting, get agreement on that, and write it into your calendar.

Take a minute to jot down ideas on which scheduling tools you might use for some of your specific tasks.

You Try It!

Things I have the most trouble keeping track of:	The tools I'll use from now on:
_____	_____
_____	_____
_____	_____
_____	_____

For information on a related topic, check out *What to Do When Everything Is Top Priority* on page 18.

Link to . . .

Handling Interruptions

Sometimes interruptions are a necessary part of the workday. At other times, interruptions are neither necessary nor welcome—the visit from a coworker that lasts too long, the news flash from the office gossip, the friend with new family pictures when you've got an impossible deadline.

The following techniques will help you to demonstrate courteously and professionally that you *really don't* have time to stop what you're doing.

- **Prevent interruptions before they begin.** Develop a no-nonsense reputation. People are far less likely to interrupt someone who takes his or her productivity seriously. If, when people interrupt you unnecessarily, you respond courteously with statements like *"I'd really like to hear about your vacation, but I'm on a tight schedule right now,"* or *"I can't talk right now, but I've got time in my schedule after 2:00,"* they soon realize that your job is important to you and they respect your time.

- **Set up a signal** that lets everyone know that this is *not* a good time for a friendly "hi," let alone a friendly chat. Examples of universal "busy signals" are:
  - Displaying a "Do Not Disturb" sign.
  - Furrowing your brow.
  - Keeping your hands on the keyboard as you say hello.
  - Glancing quickly at your watch just before you make eye contact.
  - Hesitating for just a moment before turning toward the visitor.

Most people aren't offended with these responses because they know they're not personal. They know that these are signals of a busy person who really has to stay in high gear and get things done.

- **Minimize an interruption that you can't avoid.** There are lots of ways to end a visit that's gone on (or might go on) too long. These examples will show you how a little body language can work for you.

  - Begin with a little prevention. Don't invite the visitor to sit down. Just as an invitation to sit implies that you have time to talk, the lack of an invitation implies that your time is limited.

  - If *you're* sitting, simply stand. The physical act of getting up and moving is a signal to the visitor that it's time for him or her to move along.

  - Invite the visitor to accompany you as you leave your work space. Something as simple as, *"I've got to pick up some materials in the stockroom—do you want to talk with me on the way?"* allows you to take time to help someone without creating a major disruption in your schedule. If you were planning to go to the water fountain or vending machine anyway, you might as well use the time to assist a coworker.

- **Give people options.** We're humans, not robots. There are times when you *want* to talk with someone but know that you'll be under pressure for a while. Providing alternatives lets your coworkers know that they're important to you, but you need to keep focused on your job. For example:

  - *"I can talk with you a few minutes now, or we can meet later and spend more time."*

  - *"I want to hear all about your ski trip. Can you meet me for lunch today?"*

  - *"I want to find out how your Dad's operation went. I'm between meetings at 10:30 this morning. Would it be OK if I stopped by to talk with you then?"*

Madame Make It Happen Answers All

Dear Madame Make It Happen,

I think a neat, well-organized store is important to our image, so when it's a slow time, I try to straighten things. Sometimes when I'm in the middle of straightening merchandise or stocking a new product, customers come up and ask me questions or want me to wait on them. How can I politely tell them to find someone who's not busy so I can get my work done?

Ned the Neat

Dear Ned,

I'm asked this question a lot. It feels like a sticky problem, but my crystal ball has revealed the universal answers for it:

- *Customers are NEVER an interruption.*
- *They ARE your work. Without them there is no store to fix or paperwork to complete.*
- *When in doubt, take care of the customers.*

Madame Make It Happen

Interruption Don'ts

On days when interruptions are frequent or especially bothersome, don't let them become an invitation to spin your wheels and get nowhere. Avoid this kind of unproductive thinking:

- *"Now that Les has interrupted me, I might as well have a cup of coffee and see how Jack is doing with his part of the project."*
- *"Now that I've had this many interruptions, I'll never get anything done. I might as well read all my old e-mail messages."*
- *"I've got to put up with these interruptions because I don't want people to think I'm rude."*

My major interrupters:	How I plan to deal with them:
_____	_____
_____	_____
_____	_____
_____	_____

Making Meetings Productive

Meetings are forums for communicating information, solving problems, developing new ideas, planning, and making decisions. But how often do meetings fail to meet these kinds of goals? And how does that failure affect productivity, the customer, and the bottom line? In an article about meetings, *The Wall Street Journal* reported that senior and middle managers found only 56% of their meetings to be productive. Is your experience better . . . or worse? Unproductive meetings are a common—and costly—problem for most organizations. Fortunately, this is one of the easier problems to fix.

First decide if a meeting is the best way to address your situation.

DON'T have a meeting:

- [ ] To share uncontroversial information that can be described in a memo, e-mail, or voice mail.
- [ ] To give the impression of involving people in a decision that has already been made.
- [ ] When you should really hold a performance discussion with one or two individuals.

DO have a meeting:

- [ ] When the expertise or commitment of several people is needed in order to make a decision or a plan.
- [ ] When it will save time for many people in the long run.
- [ ] If creativity is needed in order to solve a problem.

Best Practices for Meetings

■ **Always distribute an agenda before the meeting** to give people a chance to prepare.

■ **For regular team meetings, establish a standard process and format for creating the agenda** so your team doesn't have to repeatedly discuss how to do it. For example:

   − Through voice mail, e-mail, or a team bulletin board, the leader or an assigned team member should solicit agenda items before each meeting.

   − Any agenda item submitted should include a brief description, the amount of time needed to cover it, and the person's name who will lead that part of the discussion.

   − The first agenda item should be "changes or additions to the agenda." This lets you reprioritize items if needed and prevents the group from running short on time at the end if someone suddenly remembers a topic that should be discussed.

■ **Define clear roles for leadership and participation in meetings.**

   − The meeting leader should be a "facilitator"—someone who makes sure the agenda is followed in the time allowed. A facilitator does not talk the most or decide everything.

   − Every meeting should have a note taker to record decisions, agreements, next steps, or actions to be taken after the meeting. Minutes should be prepared and distributed as quickly as possible after the meeting, preferably in one to four business days.

   − Participants should arrive promptly, be prepared, contribute, and support the agenda.

■ **For regular team meetings, rotate meeting leadership duties to:**

   − Build team members' meeting leadership skills.

   − Avoid overburdening one team member with leadership duties.

   − Increase awareness of the demands of the meeting leadership role.

■ **Block out times and locations as far into the future as possible.** When people have advance notice of meetings, they can plan their work better and ensure that they can attend. If possible, hold regular meetings at the same place and time of day.

■ **Always start on time** even if all participants haven't arrived. This is the most effective way to get everyone to discipline themselves to arrive on time.

■ **Always end on time.**

Planning for a Big Event

Are you about to lead a meeting where critical decisions will be made, senior leaders will be present, or you will be under close scrutiny? Then you really need to *plan ahead* to make sure your meeting is productive and meets its goals. Here are a few pointers on things to do *before* the meeting.

☐ Schedule the meeting as far in advance as possible. Calendars of "big event" participants are usually booked weeks in advance.

☐ Interview your leader, key stakeholders, and/or expert participants to determine:

- Who should be at the meeting?
- What are the key meeting objectives?
- What are your expectations for your role and the meeting process/agenda?
- What background information must be acquired/communicated before or at the meeting?
- What could possibly go wrong, and how might you prevent it?

☐ Provide an agenda and prework, if any, at least 48 hours before the meeting. Make sure people know what they need to do to be prepared for the meeting. Send a follow-up e-mail or voice mail message alerting participants that prework is required and reminding them of the meeting place, time, and date.

☐ Make sure the room is set up. Don't use meeting time to do this.

☐ Take action if you need someone's support or are worried about unwelcome surprises during the meeting. For example, you might tell a colleague, *"Susan, I know that staffing is on everyone's mind right now, but we won't get through our agenda if people talk about it during this meeting. If it comes up, would you let people know that they'll be able to discuss it in our next meeting and request that we table the discussion for now?"*

☐ Make extra copies of the agenda and all handouts. Don't assume that people will remember to bring materials.

☐ Decide how to handle meeting processes (such as brainstorming, tracking decisions and action items, voting, etc.) so that meeting time can be spent on more productive things.

☐ Try out any presentation technology to make sure it works.

Handling Disruptive Behavior in Meetings

Behavior	What to Do
Wandering. The discussion is not focused on the purpose of the meeting, or participants stray from topic.	■ Involve participants in creating the agenda in advance so they'll agree that the topics are important. ■ Make sure agenda topics are not too broad. ■ Set time limits for discussion of each topic. ■ Make sure everyone has a copy of the agenda and make procedural suggestions to follow it. ■ Clearly state the purpose of the meeting. ■ Record off-the-subject issues for later discussion.
Bad manners. Participants come late, leave early, come and go, do other work, have side conversations, or joke around too much.	■ Hold the meeting off-site to minimize distractions. ■ Set and post ground rules about meeting behavior. ■ Include breaks so participants can make phone calls, get coffee, use the rest room, etc. ■ Hold the meeting at a time that suits everyone.
Meeting dominator. One person dominates the discussion, preventing others from participating in it.	■ Communicate a process for the meeting to follow and ask for everyone's support. ■ Propose meeting ground rules, such as airtime for everyone, no repeating what has been said, and everyone's opinion should be heard. ■ State up front the "non-purposes" of the meeting, or what participants are *not* there to discuss/decide. ■ Give feedback to the meeting dominator *before* the meeting. Here's an example: *"I know you're eager to share your opinions, but I'm not sure everyone else will be as comfortable, especially when they hear you speak with so much passion. Can you help get others to talk more?"*

Checklist for Meeting Logistics

Use the following checklist to make sure you've thought of everything for your meeting.

- ☐ Room/Amenities
    - ☐ table(s), chairs
    - ☐ room arrangement
    - ☐ electrical outlets
    - ☐ temperature regulation
    - ☐ lighting
    - ☐ phone availability
    - ☐ rest rooms
    - ☐ stairs/elevators
    - ☐ access to building/room
    - ☐ smoking area
    - ☐ parking facilities
    - ☐ wastebaskets
- ☐ Equipment/Tools
    - ☐ video monitor and player
    - ☐ flip chart(s)
    - ☐ tape recorder
    - ☐ overhead projector
    - ☐ computer
    - ☐ network hookup
    - ☐ slide projector/screen
    - ☐ extension cord(s)
    - ☐ podium
    - ☐ microphone
    - ☐ chalkboard/white board/eraser
    - ☐ paper/pencils/pens/markers
    - ☐ bulletin board
    - ☐ thumbtacks, tape
    - ☐ note cards
    - ☐ camera/film
    - ☐ try out equipment
- ☐ Refreshments
    - ☐ food/beverages
    - ☐ cups/dishes/utensils/napkins
    - ☐ coffee/tea/hot water dispenser
    - ☐ water pitchers
- ☐ Materials/Directions for participants
    - ☐ handouts/agenda copies
    - ☐ name tags
    - ☐ directions to meeting place
    - ☐ confirmation of attendance
    - ☐ previous minutes/decisions/reports
    - ☐ how to get phone messages
    - ☐ prework created/distributed
- ☐ Get myself prepared
    - ☐ check out PA system
    - ☐ preview materials
    - ☐ post flip charts/materials

Making a Basic Plan

Have you ever painted a room, repaired a home appliance, planted a garden, or hosted a party? How many trips did you make to the store to get everything you needed? If it was more than one, that's normal. Most people don't think ahead about all the items they need to complete a complex task.

People would work faster—and put fewer miles on their cars—if they created a simple plan to make sure they remember to get or do everything they should.

When to Use a Plan on the Job

You will especially benefit from a basic plan if:

- You're responsible for a job that involves multiple steps, people, or materials.
- You have a lot of things going on at once and you want to make sure nothing slips through the cracks.
- You can't do everything that needs to be done at one time because the nature of the job requires that you complete it over time. For example, if you are holding a workshop, you can't order the appropriate number of workbooks until you receive all the responses or registration forms.

What Information Should Be in a Plan?

- What needs to be done?
- What are the major steps to accomplish the job?
- What do I need to know to do the job right?
- What resources do I need to complete the job?
- Who needs to be involved, and when?
- When does it need to be done?

A Good Planning Tool

Use a worksheet to track what, when, and how you'll accomplish a job. Here's an example of a planning worksheet created by the manager of the service department in a car dealership. This person needs to organize a customer satisfaction survey.

The Job: *Telephone Survey of Our Dealership's First-Time Car Buyers* **Completion Date:** *July 11*

Done	What (List of Tasks/Steps)	Who	When	How (Information, Materials, Tools)
☐	*Create a list of survey questions.*	*Ken, Cathy, Dave, me*	*6/7 2 p.m. 2 p.m.*	*Samples from manufacturer; copies of old surveys; anecdotal customer feedback file.*
☐	*Identify customers.*	*Me*	*Week of 6/9*	*Computer database; loan applications.*
☐	*Identify callers and match to customers.*	*Cathy, Dave, Donna, me*	*Week of 6/16*	*Memo asking folks to sign up to call specific customers.*
☐	*Make calls.*	*Cathy, Dave, Donna, me*	*6/19-28 4-7 p.m.*	*Distribute copies of surveys and list of customer call sheets.*
☐	*Tabulate data.*	*Me*	*6/23-7/4*	*Collect all surveys; tabulate and compare to last 2 years' data.*
☐	*Review first draft.*	*Dave, me*	*6/26-29*	*Read printout and make suggestions to Cathy.*
☐	*Write report.*	*Cathy*	*7/11*	*Write final report, submit to Mary.*

Use this blank planning worksheet to plan one of your upcoming jobs.

You Try It!

The Job: _____ **Completion Date:** _____

Done	What (List of Tasks/Steps)	Who	When	How (Information, Materials, Tools)
☐				
☐				
☐				
☐				
☐				

Tips for Using the Planning Worksheet

- List the tasks in the order that they need to be done.

- Check off each task as you complete it.

- If other people are responsible for some of the tasks, show them a draft of the plan to keep them informed and get their buy-in. Then give them a copy of the final plan.

- If a job is delegated to you, draft a plan and share it with the person who assigned it to you. It will be a great starting point to discuss your approach. It will also give that person a chance to offer feedback on your plan and alert you to things you might not know or have forgotten.

- After the job is completed, look at the plan. What lessons did you learn? How will you do things differently as a result?

Making Contingency Plans: The Next Step

As they say, even the best-laid plans can go astray. To increase your chances of success, sometimes you need a contingency, or backup, plan—one that identifies what you'll do if your plan is disrupted. Examples of contingency plans are:

- *"If Jeff or Tim calls in sick tomorrow, I'll call in a substitute worker from this list."*
- *"If the parts don't arrive in time, we'll borrow them from the Southern Facility until the shipment comes in."*

When to Make Contingency Plans

You can't plan for every possible problem, but it's always important to ask yourself:

- What might reasonably go wrong?
- If it did go wrong, would it have a major impact on the job?
- If the impact would be significant, what can you do to prevent it?
- If you're not sure that something can be prevented, what can you do to reduce the impact if it happens?

> If something is reasonably likely to happen or will have a major impact when it does, you need to make a contingency plan.

A Practice Exercise

It's August 5. Pam is responsible for coordinating an August 19 meeting at the main plant between the shipping department and the sales reps. The purpose of the meeting is to watch a demonstration of some software that the company is considering and to get feedback from both departments. Following are some things that Pam is worried about.

1. A storm *could* hit the town, causing impassable roads and power failures.

2. Erik, the main presenter (whose wife is 8 1/2 months pregnant), *could* be unable to make it to the meeting.

3. Of the 14 salespeople, 1 or 2 *could* have an emergency call from a client and be unable to attend the meeting.

4. The 12 members of the shipping team who pool their money on payday to buy lottery tickets *could* win the jackpot and quit their jobs.

5. The computer *could* be incompatible with the software the sales rep is bringing to demonstrate at the meeting.

Below, write the numbers of the two things that are both likely and serious enough to deserve a backup plan. Once you've identified them, write one or more contingency plans that could be initiated to ensure a successful meeting. Then check your answers on the next page.

Deserves a
Contingency
Plan: _____

Possible Contingency Plan(s):

_____

_____

_____

_____

Deserves a
Contingency
Plan: _____

Possible Contingency Plan(s):

_____

_____

_____

_____

How Did You Do?

Deserves a
Contingency
Plan: _____#2_____

Possible Contingency Plan(s):
A. *Eric could choose someone to present in his place. He should give his substitute the materials and some coaching ahead of time, just in case he is called away at the last minute.*
B. *If a substitute is unavailable, the meeting could be rescheduled.*

Deserves a
Contingency
Plan: _____#5_____

Possible Contingency Plan(s):
A. *Pam could suggest that the sales rep bring paper copies of what's on the computer screens as a backup.*
B. *Pam could install and test the software on the computer the afternoon before the meeting.*

And the other choices?

Numbers 1 and 4 are too unlikely to happen, so don't worry about making contingency plans. The odds against a storm making the roads impassable or someone winning the top prize in the lottery are so high that it's not worth planning for.

Number 3 probably will happen, but the absence of one or two salespeople is unlikely to cause the cancellation of a meeting or the department's inability to make a decision. Chances are good that everyone is used to some salespeople being unable to attend a meeting.

Make contingency plans for only high-probability or high-impact possibilities.

Some of my current plans that need contingency plans are:

....

....

....

Making the Best Use of Communication Tools

Voice mail, e-mail, faxes, pagers, phone calls, memos—is there a *best* way to communicate in the Communication Age? The following tips will give you some guidelines.

Use Voice Mail When:

- The message is short and simple.

- It's got to go out fast.

- No record of the information or receipt of the message needs to be kept.

- It's good news and you want to announce it to everyone at the same time.

Use Face-to-Face Conversations When:

- The subject is sensitive or confidential.

- A memo or voice mail message could be misinterpreted.

- The situation needs a personal touch (for example, to express concern or appreciation).

Use a Written Message (E-Mail or Memo) When:

- Your message is complex or you're giving directions. For example:
    - *"To complete the new expense report, follow these steps: . . ."*
    - *"To access the software, first . . ."*

- Your message is long. Some voice mail boxes (and most busy people) will accept a limited amount in one message. When it seems that a voice mail message will go on forever, many listeners are tempted to skip through it or simply delete it.

- A record of the message needs to be kept. If you're going to type it for your files anyhow, you might as well send it as an e-mail message or memo.

- You need a receipt for a message. E-mail systems have a receipt function that alerts you when the receiver has gotten your message. When you need written verification that a message was received, you can print a receipt and put it in your files.

Understand Your Organization's Communication Climate

Your organization or department has a "communication culture"—a way to give and get information—that's unique. One of the best ways to increase your productivity is to understand how people prefer to communicate and either follow their lead or improve on it.

Use these questions to determine the best way to communicate with a coworker.

If I have a question, does _____ prefer that I:

☐ Give him or her a quick call?

☐ Leave a voice mail message?

☐ Write a memo or e-mail message?

What are the exceptions to this rule? _____

_____

If I want to make sure everyone gets my message and acts on it, my best communication method is _____.

In my work group, a paper memo means:

☐ "Read this when you have the time."

☐ "Read and respond ASAP."

Avoid Communication Blunders

- Never leave a message for someone that you wouldn't want to see published in the company newsletter.

- Never forward a sensitive voice mail without asking the originator's permission.

- Never send a memo that's going to a large or important group—especially a customer—until you've had someone else check it for mistakes and typos.

- Never use voice mail, e-mail, or memos to avoid a necessary face-to-face discussion with someone.

Creating Outgoing Voice Mail Messages

By using the following tips, you can feel confident that your voice mail messages are appreciated for their clarity and professionalism.

- **Give important information up front.** State these things in your first sentence or so:

  - Your name/department
  - The message's audience/recipients
  - The message's purpose
  - How many topics you'll cover

  - Whether a response is needed
  - A response deadline
  - Your extension
  - Whether the message is urgent

Giving folks an idea of the contents of the call lets them delete it immediately if it doesn't apply to them. (You know how annoying it is to listen to a message only to find out at the end that it doesn't affect you.)

It also helps recipients to know who else is receiving the information. (For example, if you know that a message is going to your whole team and not just to you, you know that you don't have to forward it to anyone.)

- **Think it through ahead of time.** If you have several points to make, jot them down before you begin to record your message. Then you'll remember to mention all the important points without uncomfortable pauses, babbling, or correcting yourself as you go.

- **Listen to your outgoing message BEFORE you send it.** This ensures that your message says what you intended to say. If it doesn't, change it.

- **Be straightforward, clear, and concise.** You don't have to be witty or creative when you leave a message. People appreciate your messages most when they say what needs to be said in the clearest way possible.

- **Make it easy to respond to your messages.** The following message, for example, gives the recipient little or nothing to do to get you the information you need: *"If Tuesday at 6:00 doesn't fit into your schedule, please give me a time that works better for you. If I don't hear from you by tomorrow, I'll assume it's fine, and I'll see you then."*

Leaving a Phone Message When Your Party Can't Be Reached

- **Identify yourself.** *"Hey, it's me. Gimme a call"* just isn't enough information.

- **Give the time and date of your call.** If you're not sure that the recipient's answering machine states the time and date, it's important for you to do it. This gives people a context for your message and helps to avoid confusion if you happen to end up playing phone tag. (Most company voice mail systems have a time/date feature.)

- Instead of merely asking the person to call you back, **ask the question or deliver the message.** For example:
  - *"Jack, would you please let me know the code for your incoming order."*
  - *"Jill, we have to reschedule Friday's team meeting. Would 2:00 on Monday work for you?"*

- **If the message is too complicated or personal to leave on voice mail, at least give the recipient a hint.** For example: *"I need to discuss the Peterson order with you. Please give me a call when you have the file handy and have about 10 minutes to talk."*

- **Tell the recipient when you'll be available to speak person to person.** Something like *"If you need to talk with me, I'll be at my desk between 8:00 and 10:30 tomorrow"* is just fine.

- When it's appropriate, **tell the person why you need the information.** This courtesy is likely to give the recipient some degree of buy-in with your request and net a quicker response.

- **If you need a response by a specific time, say so.** For example, *"I'll need this information when I talk with Les tomorrow afternoon. So, I'd appreciate it if you could give me a call before noon."*

- **End on a friendly note.** Something simple like *"Thanks for your time"* or *"Let me know if you have any questions"* is all you need.

Networking

Do you know who to turn to when you need information about:

☐ New products and services?

☐ Organizational changes?

☐ Customer preferences, feedback, and trends?

☐ Competitive information?

☐ Organizational policies and procedures?

☐ Job and/or promotion opportunities?

☐ Process improvements and innovations?

☐ Professional development?

Challenge yourself to seek knowledgeable contacts in each area listed above as well as others that might be more relevant to you and your organization.

Have you ever heard the cliché, "It's not what you know, it's who you know"? Sometimes it's true. In the face of rapid and continuous change, you need to keep your finger on the pulse of the organization—especially outside of your department or area of expertise.

The best way to get and stay informed is to build an effective network of reliable, knowledgeable people who are willing and able to share important information or advice.

What Networking Is

Networking can be formally defined as *the exchange of information or services among individuals, groups, or institutions.* Informally, networking means developing direct and immediate access to others within the organization who can provide practical knowledge to help you get your job done right. Think of networking as:

■ **A mutually beneficial relationship.** Each party offers unique information and experiences that the other might need for success. Think of a shark and a remora—two very different animals that need each other to survive. The shark gives the remora a free ride to meals (without making it the main course!), and the remora removes pesky parasites from the shark in return.

　　　49

- **A shared responsibility.** It's everyone's responsibility in a network to keep it alive and ensure that it's working. Partnerships require give-and-take. You need to be available to provide assistance and advice to others if you expect them to be available for you.

- **A proactive approach** to developing information inroads. A wise person once said, "It's better to know an attorney before you need one!" The same philosophy applies to networking. Seek opportunities to broaden your network now, even though you might not need to interact with some of its members until later.

What Networking Isn't

- **Just socializing.** While it doesn't hurt to make new friends or fraternize a bit (all good networkers do), the point of networking is to develop beneficial partnerships that enhance your performance and boost your productivity.

- **A one-time event.** You can't just "use 'em and lose 'em"—that's not what networking's about. Having an effective network requires regular contact and ongoing maintenance.

- **Easy.** The best things in life never are. Networking demands your initiative, time, creativity, collaboration, and discipline. All in addition to your regular responsibilities!

What Do You Want to Know?

Building networks not only will increase your visibility but also expand your knowledge base. Think of some things in your business that you'd like to know more about and consider who you might contact to find out more about it.

Things I'd like to know:	Who can tell me:

How to Make CONTACT

Concentrate on areas outside of your expertise to expand your knowledge base. Identify an area or department you should (or would like to) know more about. Pick up the phone and introduce yourself to someone in that group. Chances are that person needs to know more about what you do too!

Organize a list of potential partners based on their skills, experiences, and expertise. Give your network depth by seeking people with a variety of backgrounds, tenure, and perspectives. Keep a running list and add to it as you identify new people. This will increase the likelihood that you'll find what you need to know when you need to know it.

Nurture your network by making frequent contacts. Keep it alive. Even if you don't need to talk to Mary in production for any particular reason, give her a call or stop by once in a while just to say *"Hi! What's new?"* This will help build rapport and trust with your network affiliates.

Think about what you can offer, and promote your attributes with your partners. Find opportunities to showcase your knowledge to your network partners by sharing ideas during meetings or offering creative solutions to their problems. This will build your credibility and their confidence in you.

Acknowledge any help you receive. Show your appreciation in private and public. Even simple things can help you say *"Thank you!"* Leave a nice voice mail message to the person (and his or her manager), post a memo on a central bulletin board describing what the person did and how this action helped you, or offer to buy lunch. Not only is it common courtesy, but it will also reflect positively on you. Your networkers will notice!

Cultivate relationships by offering your expertise to others who might need it. Sometimes it can help just to say *"I've had some experience in a similar situation. Would you like to hear how I handled it?"*

Trust your contacts. Show it by what you say and do. Even the simple act of sharing pertinent information that your contacts might not be privileged to can demonstrate your trust and encourage them to do the same.

More Networking Tips

■ **Do a little detective work.** To develop an effective network with breadth and depth, you'll want to seek knowledgeable associates from every corner and cubicle of the organization. Try these approaches:

  – Scan the organizational chart to get a clear picture of how the company is structured and who works where.

  – Read company newsletters and publications. Note who is being recognized for their particular expertise.

  – Attend company-sponsored seminars and social events. This is both a fun and effective way to make contact. Make a special effort to sit next to someone you've never met before and strike up a conversation.

■ **Always carry your business cards** (if you have them). You never know who you'll run into. This is especially important as you expand your network to include people outside your organization like customers, suppliers, competitors, conference attendees, and acquaintances.

Helpful Hint

Conversely, when you receive a business card, jot some notes about that person on the back or in your card file (such as where and when you met; distinguishing features, like "bald, mustache"; and important notes from your conversation, like "considerable computer experience").

■ **Get organized.** As you make contact with new network partners, be sure to add their names (and other relevant information) to your network file or database. Keeping all your contacts organized in one area will make your network easier to maintain and access.

■ **Diversify.** Make sure that your network includes internal (team members, other departments) and external sources (customers) of information.

■ **Network your network.** Increase the reach of your network by referring your members to other people. Ask them to return the favor by referring you to others as well.

Link to . . .

Good networking techniques require good partnering skills. Check out the topics *Getting Support from Others* on page 53 and *Being a Good Partner* on page 64 for more practical tips and tools.

Getting Support from Others

Getting support from others is a fundamental business survival skill in today's ever-changing world. Several factors have increased the awareness of just how critical getting support from others can be, including:

- The growing movement toward teamwork and empowerment. Seeking and providing support is encouraged, even expected, in many organizations today.

- The need to do more with less. More and more, individuals are being asked to stretch and accept more responsibility within their current roles.

- Customer expectations continue to climb as companies "raise the bar" to deliver products and services cheaper, better, and faster.

Madame Make It Happen Answers All

Madame Make It Happen,

I like to do things on my own and usually avoid asking for help. I don't want anyone to think that I'm incompetent or incapable of doing the job. Is there a way I can ask for support without raising any doubts?

Sincerely,
A Friend in Need

Dear Friend,

We all need help at one time or another. And seeking support is a positive approach to meeting practical business needs. People will appreciate your honesty and admire your concern for getting the job done right the first time as a result of your wisdom and willingness to set aside your ego. Just remember to use your judgment as you consider when, who, and how you ask for support.

Yours truly,

Madame M.

Caution

Be judicious and don't "cry wolf." Don't try to get help for every little thing. Ask for help only when you really need it, and you'll be more likely to get it.

When to Seek Support

You might need support from others when you want or need to:

☐ Learn faster. This is especially important as you approach new or challenging assignments that need to be done quickly and accurately. Finding more experienced people to help you fill in the gaps can flatten your learning curve and help you get the job done swiftly.

☐ Decrease the likelihood of mistakes and rework. When you are working under tight deadlines, you barely have time to do things right, let alone to do them over again! Learn from others' mistakes and war stories rather than making your own.

☐ Boost your expertise. Increase your value to the organization by learning as much as possible about the people and processes that make it a success. Study "the pros" by observing them in action and actively seeking their coaching and support.

Helpful Hint

As you ask for help, remember that you are still ultimately responsible for getting the job done. Don't ask or expect anyone else to be accountable for your work.

☐ Fulfill your current commitments, but are in danger of missing a deadline. Don't wait until you're buried by an unmanageable workload before you seek much-needed relief. Ask for help at the first signs of trouble.

Who to Ask for Support

Link to . . .

■ **Put your network to work.** If you've done a good job establishing and maintaining your network, you should have a pool of internal and external partners ready, willing, and able to lend you a hand in your time of need. (You'll find more on related subjects in *Networking* on page 49.)

- **Ask your boss, who (usually) knows best.** Although he or she might not be the best person to actually help, your boss should be able to point you in the right direction. Given his or her organizational position and experience, your boss probably has a better understanding of what resources are available as well as the "pull" to help you obtain them.

- **Tap your team.** If you're part of a team, you probably already enjoy the luxury of instant support from your teammates. However, at times you might need more help than usual. Your teammates know you well and should be able to roll up their sleeves and get to work quickly with little "ramp up" time or explanation.

- **Survey your suppliers.** When you have established relationships with particular suppliers, they might support you by enhancing their level of service or recommending other suppliers. Successful suppliers can also act as good benchmark companies. Note their best practices as you work with them.

The Etiquette of Asking for Support

Link to . . .

There are two ways to ask for support: the right way and the wrong way. To ensure that you get the help you need, when you need it, you'll want to observe the etiquette of asking for support. (You'll find related information in ***Being a Good Partner*** on page 64.)

- **Ask early.** Don't wait until your house is on fire to ask your neighbor to help you install a smoke detector. Give yourself and your helper enough time to adjust your schedules and do what needs to be done.

- **Don't take help for granted.** You're the one who needs help; you're in no position to make demands. You are requesting that someone take time away from his or her own busy schedule to lend you a hand. Show respect for your partners by sharing how much you value their time and their help.

- **Be specific about what you need help with.** Provide as much detail as you can up front, including what you hope to accomplish, how much time it will take, and what's been done so far. Being clear from the start will cut the amount of time spent re-explaining things further down the road.

- **Be honest about what's involved.** Don't make it sound easier than it is just to entrap a hapless helper. If it will mean working late, say so, even though it might make the person decide not to help. If you withhold such important information, you'll diminish trust when your helper eventually finds out, and you'll damage your relationship.

- **Throw a few lines in the water and hope you get at least one bite.** You might not get help from the first person you ask, so float your opportunity by more than one person and hope you get at least one offer of help.

Helpful Hint

If you end up with more than one "taker," consider each volunteer's other responsibilities and the number of times you've sought support from him or her in the past. Be sure to notify all the volunteers once you've chosen one so they don't waste time unnecessarily rearranging their schedules.

- **Support your supporter.** It's still your job—you know it best. Ensure a successful partnership by being available to answer questions or to provide any coaching if your worthy volunteer needs it.

- **Don't use false flattery to secure support.** While you should highlight your helper's strengths and how they can be utilized to assist you, don't overdo it. Be sincere and complimentary without making the other person feel like he or she is being manipulated or tricked into helping you.

Show Your Appreciation

If you're fortunate enough to find help, do whatever you can to keep it! Your sincere gratitude, whether formal or informal, will encourage people to support you again on future projects. Expressions of appreciation are always appreciated!

- **Put it in writing.** Write a note or e-mail message of acknowledgment. Offer positive reinforcement on the support you've received by sharing specific feedback. Be sure to include details regarding the situation, what the person did to provide support, and what happened as a result of the helper's efforts.

- **Make the call.** Pick up the phone and call your partner. This is a more informal but often more personal approach to showing your appreciation. If you want to be more formal, leave a detailed voice mail message about the good work that's been done. Send it to your partner and copy anyone else who should hear it (like his or her boss).

- **Copy any formal thanks** and feedback that you provide **to that person's boss** and spread the word about his or her willingness and ability to help. Keep your boss informed by adding him or her to the distribution list when you send out thank-you voice mail or e-mail messages.

- **Knock on the door.** The most personal way to thank someone is face to face. If you're feeling generous, offer to buy lunch as a way of thanking the person for helping in your time of need. Your partner will remember this kind, seemingly small act the next time you need support.

- **Give as you receive.** One of the most effective ways to enlist the support of others is to provide (or sincerely offer to provide) reciprocal support. The more you work together and support each other, the stronger your relationship will become.

Helpful Hint

No matter how you choose to share it, make sure the feedback that you give to your partner is both timely and sincere. Don't wait until two months after the completion of the task or project to say *"Thank you."*

Making Clear Agreements

How many times has something like this happened to you? Come on, admit it. At least once we've all found ourselves on a sinking ship, slogging through a sea of confusion as a result of some unfortunate—and certainly unintentional—misunderstanding.

It seems like we're all in such a hurry to solve problems, make key decisions, and get the job done that we often rush right by deciding *how* we're going to do these things, *who's* going to do them, and *when* they should be done. Have you ever experienced any of the following as a result:

☐ Missed deadlines or rework?

☐ Important details falling through the cracks?

☐ Working longer and harder to make up for lost time?

☐ Increased stress levels?

☐ Diminished confidence and trust between you and your partners?

You might experience any or all of these undesirable outcomes if and when you and your coworkers fail to make clear agreements.

What Causes Unclear Agreements

Assumptions . . . everyone makes them at one time or another. When you think you know everything, why bother to check and see if you're right, right? The problem is that assumptions—in some way, shape, or form—are at the heart of nearly all unclear agreements. Do you ever make assumptions about:

- The meaning of terms? *"I thought we agreed that this would be a 'high-quality' product."*

- Role clarity? *"That's the salespeople's job to talk to the customer—not mine."*

- Other people's motivation or attitudes? *"That department doesn't care about meeting deadlines or cutting expenses."*

- Other people's knowledge or awareness? *"That's been the policy for years. . . . She should've known that."*

- Other people's priorities? *"Dave doesn't have enough work to keep him busy. Give the project to him."*

Proactively Setting the Stage to Ensure Clear Agreements

When you first begin working with others on a new project or assignment, take some time to formulate acceptable guidelines outlining how you'll work together, what you'll accomplish, what processes you'll follow, what terms you'll use, who will be responsible for what, and what standards of behavior will be expected. This preparation will help you create new "assumptions" that everyone can agree to and act in accordance with.

The following tips provide examples of opportunities to proactively set guidelines to create a shared understanding with others and avoid unclear agreements in the future.

- **Clearly state the purpose, importance, and expected outcome.** If everyone understands what is to be accomplished and why, you'll create a context for any future agreement. It will also give people the knowledge necessary to interpret agreements more accurately and to identify when they need to check their understanding. For example: *"It sounded like Richard wants us to work overtime. Since we're trying to keep costs down, it's possible that I misunderstood what he meant. I'd better check."*

- **Clarify roles and responsibilities.** Using a role clarity chart, outline exactly what each person (including yourself) will be responsible for. Specify the formal or informal role you and your partners will play with regard to the project, assignment, or team. Be sure to discuss boundaries of authority and approval processes, as needed.

Remember that roles and responsibilities change from time to time, so don't assume that someone will take on a task that he or she has handled before. Check first.

Helpful Hint

Sample Role Clarity Chart

Task: *Prepare report for management meeting next month.*

Role	Description	Individual
Coordinator/Coach	*Works with the management meeting leader, report writer, and reviewers to coordinate the timely production of the report. Coaches other team members regarding meeting participant expectations.*	*Chris*
Report writer	*Designs and develops the report. Incorporates feedback from reviewers and produces the final draft by the specified deadline.*	*Tony*
Reviewers	*Review and provide feedback on all report drafts. Are available for brainstorming and are willing to provide coaching and support as needed. Approve the final report.*	*John and Jeff*

- **Establish ground rules.** Establish some basic rules to clearly communicate the standards of behavior that are expected. Some common ones:
  - Address disagreements directly with those involved (no circumventing).
  - Treat one another with respect.
  - Meet commitments.
  - Be willing to give and accept feedback on job performance.
  - Make decisions by consensus when possible.

- **Clarify boundaries of authority.** Ask probing questions to help you avoid potential "turf wars" or misunderstandings by clarifying boundaries for everyone involved. For example:
  - *"What kinds of decisions do or do not need approval?"*
  - *"Who are our customers, and what are their requirements?"*
  - *"Who must we involve in or inform of our progress?"*
  - *"How will we involve or inform others? How often?"*
  - *"Who is the 'buck stopper' if consensus cannot be reached on a particular issue?"*

Strategies for Making Clear Agreements

Even if you've proactively set the stage for success, sometimes during the course of a conversation, an unclear agreement slips by. Minimize misunderstandings by using the following strategies for making clear agreements.

1. **Clarify terms** that you or someone else might not understand. Not everyone will ask for a definition or explanation. No one wants to admit to being confused or appear uninformed, even if you expect it to happen. Save people the embarrassment by using more common terms, offering explanations, or simply checking for understanding. For example, *"Does everyone know what I mean by JIT? For those of you who don't, JIT, or just in time, is a process by which . . ."*

Caution

Watch out for misunderstandings involving supposedly common terms. For example, *"When you say the product is 'ready,' do you mean that it's ready to be packaged or ready to be shipped?"*

2. **Take good notes** and encourage others to do the same. Many times agreements aren't honored because people simply forget what they've agreed to. Avoid this problem by designating a note taker or action tracker to capture all key decisions on a flip chart so that everyone involved can see how the agreements are being recorded. This will give everyone a chance to ask questions or suggest revisions to the agreement(s).

3. **Commit it to paper** once you've made a clear agreement. Make a table to specify details of who will do specific actions by when. This will reduce the risk of future misunderstandings and build the group's feelings of ownership over and commitment to the project.

Who	What	By When	Additional Resources
Alice	*Set up and facilitate meeting with Carl and Erica to make final revisions to the plan.*	*12/3*	*Lisa—Can schedule a conference room.*

4. **Check for understanding.** One way to ensure that everyone involved in the discussion has agreed to the same thing is to simply paraphrase what has been said and ask if you've understood correctly. For example, ask, *"Do we agree that the best way to tackle the problem is to split into sub-teams and . . ."*

5. **Measure your success.** Once you've made an agreement, be sure to follow up and measure your progress toward your goals. If the task requires a lot of time or resources, have periodic updates to ensure that you accomplish your agreed-upon goals by the deadline.

Addressing Agreement Issues

A wise person once said, "You can't please all the people all the time." That's a real truth when it comes to making clear agreements. Here are a few helpful hints to consider as you encounter challenging agreement discussions.

■ Sometimes people don't feel good about an agreement; however, they need to adhere to it. If this is the case, acknowledge their feelings and confirm their commitment. For example, say, *"Tom, I know this isn't the direction you expected the project to go and that you're frustrated. I just want to check that you're confident you can complete the assignment according to the schedule."*

- Build in some mechanisms in the event that people find out they can't keep their part of the agreement. *"If anyone anticipates any problems with the agreement we made, get back to me or the team as soon as you suspect there could be a problem."*

- If, in spite of your best efforts, agreements aren't understood, try to put a positive spin on the experience by learning from mistakes. Ask, *"Where did our agreement break down? How can we prevent something like this from happening again in the future?"*

Ensuring that agreements are fulfilled is a shared responsibility. Follow up appropriately with your partners and teammates to complete agreed-upon goals by the dates and times promised.

Link to . . .

For related information, have a look at *Effective Follow-Up* on page 68.

Being a Good Partner

Interdependence is a way of life in today's process-oriented workplace, and partnerships and productivity go hand in hand. You and your internal partners rely on one another to provide timely information, ideas, services, solutions, decisions, and feedback. And as often as you might seek support, you will be asked to provide it. That is, if others consider you to be a "good partner." So, how do you know if you're a good partner?

Are You a Good Partner?

Read each statement and check the box that you believe most accurately describes how others perceive you as a partner.

	Rarely	Sometimes	Often
People say, *"I can count on you. You always do what you say you'll do."*	☐	☐	☐
People describe you as skilled and knowledgeable in your area of expertise.	☐	☐	☐
When others are asked, *"Who would you like to work with on this?"* your name always comes up.	☐	☐	☐
You are known as a person who admits mistakes, promptly corrects them, and tries to keep from repeating them.	☐	☐	☐
Partners say, *"I'm never caught by surprise. You always keep me informed."*	☐	☐	☐
You are willing and able to help others when needed.	☐	☐	☐
You try to learn as much as you can about your partner's job and role in the organization. You acknowledge others' contributions and share any recognition you receive for a job well done.	☐	☐	☐
You deal with problems honestly and directly.	☐	☐	☐

Get SMART—Tips for Being a Good Partner

One of the most important things you can do to increase your credibility is to show your commitment to your partners through your actions and words.

Share information and ideas. As a good partner, you can support shared goals by:

- Offering innovative ideas as you approach new and challenging tasks.
- Sharing information that your partners might not be aware of.
- Voicing concerns based on past experiences in an effort to avoid future problems.

Make commitments you can keep. Do what you promised to do when you promised to do it. This will build your partners' confidence and trust in you. If you are unable to meet a commitment, alert your partners as soon as possible and provide options, resources, and recommendations for fulfilling your commitment.

Address conflicts quickly and directly. You and your partners won't agree on everything (and you shouldn't!). When a conflict arises, good partners:

- Discuss differences *with* one another instead of talking *about* one another.
- Maintain one another's self-esteem rather than attacking or accusing.
- Listen to and share new ideas to resolve the conflict.
- Don't hold grudges.

Request and accept feedback. No partnership can be successful without two-way communication. Good partners initiate and encourage the feedback-sharing process by asking simple questions such as *"How did I do?"* or *"What could I have done differently?"* They also offer feedback by saying things like *"If you have a few minutes, I'd like to share some feedback with you. I was really impressed with your presentation, especially . . ."*

Test assumptions. While it's not a good idea to make assumptions in the first place, everyone is guilty of it. Good partners recognize when they're making an assumption and stop to check it out. Seek all the information you can to confirm or deny your suspicions and run it by your partners for good measure.

Partnering Don'ts

Productive partners are careful not to:

- Overcommit or break commitments.
- Waste other people's time.
- Interrupt others too often when they're working.
- Take sole credit for joint work.
- Blame their partners when things go wrong.
- Guess at motives or make assumptions.
- Be partner-oriented only when they need help.

Building Better Partnerships

Effective partnerships take time to develop, and the results are well worth the effort as you and your partners become more productive together. Here are a few more tips to ensure your success.

- Work together to establish ground rules for working together. Examples of rules are "Share responsibility for successes and setbacks" and "Ask questions first rather than making assumptions."

- Set up a clarifying meeting focused on what "quality" means to each of you. If you can agree on a common definition or understanding of what a "high-quality job" is, you'll avoid future conflicts or confusion.

- "Shadow" your partners to learn more about their roles. By spending time with partners as they perform their jobs, you'll get a better understanding of their daily routines, the challenges they face, the technical language they speak, and how you affect their productivity. Extend an invitation to your partners to spend time with you on the job.

- Update one another regularly on current projects and future needs. This way, you and your partners are less likely to be caught by surprise.

- Schedule occasional meetings to reflect on the partnership. Exchange feedback on what's going well and discuss opportunities to improve the partnership. Use these simple questions to guide the discussion:
  - *"What should I stop doing?"*
  - *"What should I start doing differently?"*
  - *"What am I doing well that I should continue to do?"*

- Create a partnership scorecard to enhance the feedback process. Your scorecard can help you evaluate areas essential to the partnership's success, including communication, responsiveness, respect, and support, to mention a few. Provide a rating scale to make measurement easier as you reflect on your partners' behavior and your own. Schedule scorecard checks around project milestones to share ratings and improvement ideas.

Partner's Name:	Partnership Scorecard	Your Name:
_____	**SAMPLE**	_____
1 2 3 4		1 2 3 4
☐ ☐ ☐ ☐	**Communication**—Listens and checks for my/our understanding. Exchanges relevant and reliable information in a clear and appropriate manner.	☐ ☐ ☐ ☐
☐ ☐ ☐ ☐	**Continuous improvement**—Checks my/our level of satisfaction. Improves by seeking our input and responding to feedback.	☐ ☐ ☐ ☐
☐ ☐ ☐ ☐	**Respect**—Understands and values my/our role, responsibilities, and contributions.	☐ ☐ ☐ ☐

- Set goals for acknowledging your partners. For example, you might set a goal of sending a thank-you e-mail or voice mail message at least once per quarter to let your partners know what they're doing well while expressing your sincere appreciation and gratitude.

You'll find more information on related subjects in the following sections: *Networking* on page 49 and *Getting Support from Others* on page 53.

Link to . . .

Effective Follow-Up

Follow-up is a well-developed skill practiced by the most productive people. This skill is particularly important if you:

☐ Rely on other people to help you get your work done.

☐ Need to work frequently with other people in the organization to achieve common goals and objectives.

☐ Regularly delegate routine tasks or assignments.

If you checked any of these boxes, then you've turned to the right topic. Good follow-up skills can help you work more productively with others as well as enhance your own performance. The key is in knowing how and when you should do it.

A Delicate Balance

Just as you can't toss a few seeds into the ground and expect to have a fruitful garden, you can't make agreements or delegate assignments and simply hope they will happen. Left untended, your projects might die on the vine, as other people's priorities—like encroaching weeds— begin to take precedence over your own.

If you want to ensure that your tasks and assignments get completed on time, you need to follow up regularly with those involved in making sure the job gets done. So what does "regularly" mean?

Caution

There's a fine line between follow-up and overkill. Imagine what would happen if you watered your plants every day. Now, imagine if you followed up every day with the people who have committed to complete some task or project for you. Different scenarios, same result—wilted, waterlogged, and unmotivated plants and people. So how do you achieve that delicate balance between "letting go" and "staying close"?

The Do's and Don'ts of Following Up

DO	DON'T
■ Clearly describe *what* needs to be accomplished, including any guidelines on *how* it must be done.	■ Give vague guidance and then later blame the other person(s) for "not doing it right."
■ Agree on a follow-up approach in advance, including how you'll update and how often. Then you won't be checking up on anyone unexpectedly or inappropriately.	■ Follow up every 10 minutes or every 10 weeks to see how things are going and to offer support.
■ Establish specific milestones to check progress regularly.	■ Wait until the last minute to check on progress.
■ Use appropriate communication tools to follow up, such as e-mail, voice mail, faxes, etc.	■ Use a communication tool that is likely to be overlooked (such as a memo to someone who travels a lot).
■ Work together in advance to develop contingency plans or ways to get back on track if things start to fall behind.	■ Blame or berate someone for being honest about his or her lack of progress.

DO	DON'T
■ Follow up on activities appropriate to you.	■ Make the other person do all the following up.
■ Schedule regular update meetings or discussions.	■ Assume that everything's going according to plan and that "no news is good news."
■ Recognize and celebrate major and minor milestones. Thank and acknowledge people when they meet their commitments.	■ Take the good work and run! Or, worse yet, take credit for a job well done by others.

You'll find more on related subjects in ***Making the Best Use of Communication Tools*** on page 45.

Link to . . .

More Tips for Effective Follow-Up

■ Be available to provide support when people need you, without hovering over anybody's shoulder. Encourage them to let you know when they need your help or expertise.

■ Supplement your formal follow-up with a more casual approach by making it part of your daily routine. If you meet by the coffee machine, take the opportunity to ask *"So, how's it coming with . . . ?"* You can also use these opportunities to acknowledge any progress you already know about.

■ If either of you feels unsure about how the assignment will proceed, set up more frequent follow-up discussions. If the work progresses nicely, you can cut back on the frequency.

■ If the assignment is not progressing as you had agreed and hoped, encourage a discussion of what is causing the delay or problem and work together to overcome it.

The Tool: Follow-Up Checklist

Task/Assignment: *Tabulate customer survey results*   **Partner:** *JoAnn*   **Deadline:** *12/3*

Done	Do by:	Follow-Up Action
☐	*10/7*	1. *Stop by JoAnn's cubicle to review customer survey (raw data) and discuss approach for tabulating results.*
☐	*10/15 or 10/20*	2. *Review JoAnn's first drafts of the graphs, charts, and tables to make sure we agree about the "look" before she gets too far along.*
☐	*10/27*	3. *Leave a voice mail and see if I can do anything to help JoAnn with graphs, charts, and tables.*
☐	*11/01*	4. *JoAnn to have finished graphs, charts, and tables.*
☐	*11/15*	5. *Mid-month status check.*
☐	*11/29*	6. *If I haven't heard from JoAnn about her portion of the presentation needed 12/3 for photocopying, call or stop by to see if I can help.*

Helpful Hint

Use your calendar or day planner to jot down these kinds of notes on the days that you want to follow up so that you don't forget.

Put together a follow-up checklist for each of your major tasks or responsibilities in order to remind yourself of what's been agreed to and when to follow up.

You Try It!

Task/Assignment: _____ Partner: _____ Deadline: _____

Done	Do by:	Follow-Up Action
☐		
☐		
☐		
☐		
☐		
☐		
☐		

For more information on a related topic, turn to *Making Clear Agreements* on page 58.

Link to . . .

Keeping Yourself Motivated in Tough Times

Your job skills aren't the only things that influence your productivity. There is a direct correlation between your feelings and your performance. People who feel energized and happy about their jobs are likely to be more productive. People who are upset, frustrated, and unmotivated find it hard to do a good job, much less a great one.

If you aren't feeling good about your work situation, read on to see how you can manage feelings such as boredom, burnout, and dissatisfaction.

The Approach: Reframe the Game

An attitude change alters more than your attitude. Scientists have found that modifying how you look at something actually changes how your body and mind react to it. By changing how you think, you can truly change:

■ How you feel.

■ How your body reacts to circumstances.

■ What you are able to do in a given situation.

■ The decisions you make about the future.

Reframing the Game means looking at the same old reality from a different point of view. Instead of dwelling on all the things you dislike about your current situation and allowing those thoughts and feelings to drag you down, reframing is about looking at positive parts of the situation (or finding ways to make it better) and letting those positive feelings and thoughts support you.

Consider the old example of two people who look at a half-filled glass of water. The pessimist sees the glass as half empty; the optimist, half full. It's the same glass with the same amount of water, but perspective changes everything.

Reframing the game doesn't mean just telling yourself to be happy or blindly accepting your lot. It's a three-step process that helps you to change what you can and to find the best in what you cannot change.

Step 1. Clearly identify why you're feeling bad. Pinpoint what part of your situation bothers you. Sometimes when you look closely, you find that just one or two specific things are demotivating you, not the whole job. Use the checklist below to identify specifically what demotivates you. Add your own ideas in the spaces provided.

Reasons I'm unmotivated in my current job or situation:

- ☐ My job doesn't provide enough variety.
- ☐ I'm always feeling overwhelmed.
- ☐ I don't enjoy the people I work with.
- ☐ I can't seem to work with my boss.
- ☐ I'm not challenged enough.
- ☐ I feel I have no control over this situation.

- ☐ _____
- ☐ _____

Step 2. Decide what to do about the parts that _can_ change. Are there _parts_ of the job that can change? The answer is probably "Yes." You might need to be creative, be persistent, or go against "the way it's always been," but if you can show that a change benefits your organization, you often can get support for it. Here's an example.

Gwen, an administrative assistant in a real estate office, was in an apparent no-win situation. As she tried to complete one associate's request, another would interrupt her with a more pressing one. Whether she stopped what she was doing and satisfied the second person or kept working on the first job and satisfied the first person, someone was always angry with her. She was ready to quit when she decided to ask her boss to give her idea a try.

Now Gwen has a large white board beside her desk on which everyone writes their requests. When people have an emergency request, it's their responsibility to check with the person they want to "bump" to get their job done out of turn. Now that the entire group sees what she's doing and shares in the scheduling, Gwen can set priorities that make sense to everyone. And suddenly, because the list is public, there are far fewer emergencies.

Step 3. With the unchangeable, shift your focus. Some things can't be changed. If you're a salmon fisherman, you probably must put up with the fact that your working conditions will be cold and wet. If you're a waiter, you probably have to deal with demanding customers. That's reality.

In Step 3, focus on what you can do to change your *reactions* to the situation. Think of how you can reframe the job to make it more interesting, challenging, or simply acceptable by shifting your focus to the positive parts of the job, to your options, or to how you can reward yourself for hanging in there.

The first shift is from demotivating thinking to motivating thinking. In this shift, think of ways you can change your perception of the job, either by changing your thinking or your future.

The First Shift

From Demotivating:	To Motivating:
I can't stand this job.	*There are some good parts of this job. What parts do I like? Are there ways that I can do more of the good parts?*
I'm overwhelmed. I'll never get this done!	*What part of the job can I get done now? Who can give me coaching on a different approach to this job that might make it more manageable?*
The repetition is boring.	*What part of the job is boring? What part of this job can I make into a game? How can I challenge myself to do the repetitious stuff better, faster, more creatively?*
I'm capable of handling a more responsible job.	*This isn't the job of my dreams, but it's what I have to do to learn the ropes in the organization. I'm willing to put up with this now because of what it will mean in the future.*

From Demotivating:	To Motivating:
I don't feel respected in this job.	*Am I being too sensitive? Am I respecting others? What can I do to earn other people's respect?*
I don't feel that people appreciate my contributions to the team.	*How can I make sure my contributions are on the mark? How can I promote my contributions? How can I advertise my accomplishments?*
I can't seem to work with my boss.	*What can my boss and I do together to clarify job priorities and expectations? What can I do to build my boss' respect for me?*
I'm going to be stuck here forever!	*What steps can I take to move on to something I **really** like?* *— Do I need more education?* *— More experience?* *Who might be able to give me information or help? What would my first steps be?*
There's not enough variety in this job.	*Is there a coworker who might trade an assignment with me so I can try something new? Can I ask my boss for a "stretch" assignment in an area I'm interested in?*
By the end of the day, I'm always overwhelmed.	*What can I do to sharpen my organizational skills? Can I develop a more efficient process that would lessen the chaos?*

There could be times that these changes and options aren't enough to keep your spirits up and your productivity consistently high. When this happens, take charge of your outlook by rewarding yourself for doing a good job. Shift from focusing on the problem to giving yourself rewards.

The Second Shift

<table>
<tr><td>**From the Problem:**</td><td>**To the Rewards:**</td></tr>
<tr>
<td>*I'm not going to have any time for myself until this project is done.*</td>
<td>*When I get **this piece** of the job done, what can I do to reward myself? What plans can I make with a friend— lunch, movie, tennis game—that will give me a break even while I'm on this project? What can I do to leave the job responsibilities with the job when I leave work? Who can remind me to keep doing this?*</td>
</tr>
<tr>
<td>*I'm always exhausted.*</td>
<td>*I'm going to plan for someone to pick up the responsibilities at home that I dislike the most—yard work, ironing, grocery shopping—just for the next week. I'm going to carve an hour of uninterrupted time for myself on these stressful days to unwind with a hot bath, a good book, or a massage.*</td>
</tr>
<tr>
<td>*I have to put in so much overtime.*</td>
<td>*Part of my overtime pay is going to go for something I've really wanted for a long time—a vacation, a computer, some new CDs.*</td>
</tr>
</table>

Now it's your turn to shift your focus. Think of something that feels demotivating about your current job. Then fill in the blanks with new ways that you can "Reframe the Game."

You Try It!

Shift From

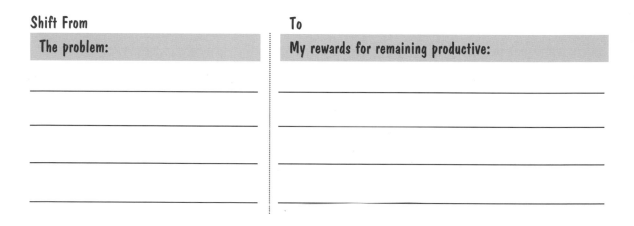

The demotivating situation/thinking:	The actions I'll take to increase my motivation:

To

Shift From

The problem:	My rewards for remaining productive:

To

For other information that relates to this topic, check out *Organizing Your Work Area* on page 25, *Keeping Track of Your Time and Tasks* on page 28, or *Making a Basic Plan* on page 39.

Link to . . .

Recognizing and Avoiding Perfectionism

Dear Emmy,

Doing an excellent, even perfect, job is not necessarily perfectionism. Some jobs require a lot of precision. No one wants a carpenter who's an inch or two off when he's making table legs, an accountant whose balance sheet is a little off, or an administrative assistant who misses some typos.

Perfectionism comes into play when a carpenter refuses to finish the table because the grain in the wood isn't to his liking, when an accountant turns in her reports late because she doesn't like the way the tables look, or when an administrative assistant reformats a memo six times while looking for the "perfect" font.

Perfectionism usually involves a fuss factor. And it usually involves "me" more than the job. For example:

- *"Yes, I know you think I'm just being fussy, but that's the way I am."*
- *"Others can be satisfied with OK, but I know I'm capable of being much better."*
- *"I don't want my name on that project if I can't have enough time to make it as good as I can."*
- *"I'd be embarrassed to admit that I'm not as good at this as I should be."*

For more information about the problems with perfectionism, check out the rest of this section.

Madame Make It Happen

A Quick Check

Think you might be a perfectionist? Put a check by the descriptions that fit you.

☐ You don't ask for help because no one can do the job as well as you can.

☐ You have a to-do list full of half-finished projects.

☐ You care about your projects more than everyone else cares about theirs.

☐ You know that if you had a little more time, you could have gotten it just right.

☐ You don't start things you might like to do because you fear you won't do them well enough.

What Perfectionism Is, and Is Not

■ Perfectionism IS believing that 100% perfect is the only acceptable standard and that anything less is of no value.

■ Perfectionism IS an all-or-nothing state of mind.

■ Perfectionism IS about thinking that every task or assignment has equal importance, when, in fact, some have more weight than others.

■ Perfectionism IS NOT about trying to do a good job or meeting your customer's needs.

Look at the next page to see how perfectionists' perceptions differ from other people's.

Fantastic!	It's OK
Great job	Needs more work
Good job	Still not good
I'm getting better	Why do I bother?
Not too bad	I'm not good at this
Gotta try harder	Terrible

How most people view their performance

How perfectionists view their performance

Take a Hard Look

To align your sights on quality with the views of your organization, internal partners, and customers, ask yourself or others (your customers, leader, and team members) the following questions.

- Do my customers/leader/team members think that the extra time and effort I put into making something perfect is worthwhile?
- Do I do the best I can in the allotted time?
- Do I miss my deadlines in my attempt to make things better?
- If someone else had done this work, would I think it is acceptable for them?
- Do I do so many progress checks that I stop progress?
- Do I add extra touches that don't really improve the quality of the product or service?
- Does the extra time I spend to make something just a little better really add to the quality?
- What could I do to ensure good quality with less time and fuss?
- Have people refused to work with me because I spend too much time and energy on things that don't matter to the rest of the team?

Adjust Your Definition of a Good Job

Once you understand how others in your organization view quality, it's time to change your driving motto to "Quality, Not Perfection."

"Quality, Not Perfection" does not mean doing a sloppy job or turning out a flawed product. It means accepting the fact that if a job meets your customer's definition of quality, it's a job well done. Seeking quality means:

- Accepting that your personal touches might not add value in the eyes of the customer.
- Accepting that alternative ways to do something could work as well as your own.
- Understanding that function and quality aren't always defined by how a product looks or which product has the most "bells and whistles."

Tips for Making "Quality, Not Perfection" Part of Your Work Life

- Ask questions up front to define how good is good enough.
  - *"What are the expected results of this job?"*
  - *"Should I put the information into a formal report or in an outline form?"*
  - *"When do you need this information?"*
  - *"Do you need a rough estimate or a detailed breakdown?"*
  - *"Would a verbal reply be OK, or do you need a formal memo?"*
  - *"Are there acceptable shortcuts that I can take?"*
  - *"What if I stopped right now?"*
- Ask for samples.
  - *"Could you show me a sample of what a good widget looks like?"*
  - *"Could I see a copy of a report that filled your needs?"*
  - *"Do you have an example of the kind of schedule you're looking for?"*
- Check your assumptions.
  - *"I assume that you'll want the figures for the entire fiscal year in the report. Is that right?"*
  - *"I've got orders from half of Thompson's sales reps. I assume I wait for all of them before I begin to fill the shipment. Is that right?"*

- Give others permission to coach or challenge you if they notice you're becoming too perfectionistic.
    - *"Leslie, please feel free to tell me if I'm being too picky about style issues."*
    - *"George, please help me to understand the best way to prepare this report for Ross. Does he prefer to see a quick first draft or a polished final draft?"*
- Check direction as you go.
    - *"This step will add three days to the project. Is the result/impact/improvement important enough to add three more days?"*
    - *"I could reformat this report into bullet points to make it easier to read. Would that be worthwhile?"*

For information on a related topic, check out ***Examining Your Priorities*** on page 14.

Link to . . .

Nonthreatening Ways to Practice "Quality, Not Perfection"

Getting rid of perfection is a hard and sometimes scary job. It might be easier to risk being less than perfect if you practice first off the job (or on the job when you feel you have little to risk). Try a couple of these suggestions:

- Do something—a game, a sport, a dance, a musical instrument, painting—especially when you know you'll never be the greatest.
- Don't redo the work of your children, spouse, or friends, even if it falls short of how you would do it.
- Stop yourself before you revise, rework, rearrange, or re-anything a task that's low in importance or urgency.
- Dare to risk making mistakes—and allow yourself to learn from them.

I can take the risk of being less than perfect by:

....

....

....

Steps I'm going to take to overcome my perfectionism on the job:

....

....

....

....

....

As you become less perfectionistic in small areas (and find you're a pretty nifty person even if you're not perfect), you'll be free to be less demanding of yourself and others on the job.

Dare to be an "imperfectionist." It's usually much more productive!

Conquering Procrastination

Why do people procrastinate?

To avoid the pain of doing something they don't want to do.

Does procrastination work?

Most of the time, it doesn't. Procrastination usually causes more pain in the long run.

So why do you keep putting things off until later?

Maybe once, when you procrastinated, someone else did your job for you. Or another time, you procrastinated for so long that the situation changed, and you didn't have to do the thing you were avoiding. That's enough reason for most people.

How can you beat procrastination?

If you really want to tackle procrastination, you must take a two-part approach: manage the *job* and manage *yourself*. Let's start with the easier of the two—managing the job.

Managing the Job—The Procrastination Basher

The Procrastination Basher is a tool that helps you to manage a job that seems insurmountable by using the following three steps.

1. **Break the job into doable tasks.** Remember the joke from your childhood, "How can an ant swallow an elephant?" The answer: "One bite at a time." Just make sure your "bites" are specific and practical.

2. **Set a reasonable deadline for each task.** The secret here is to make the deadlines reasonable enough so that you don't set yourself up for failure, yet challenging enough so that you continue to make progress.

3. **Track your progress.** When a job is unpleasant, people often fool themselves into thinking that they're doing more than they actually are. Simply tracking what you've done and holding yourself accountable for meeting your commitments will dramatically increase your productivity.

The Procrastination Basher in Action

George has been assigned the job of installing and getting the people on his team up to speed on some new groupware—software that allows an entire department to do centralized scheduling and project tracking. He's been procrastinating because he's never done anything like this before and isn't sure how to do it.

George used the Procrastination Basher to break the job into chunks, each with a deadline. He asked for coaching from a coworker who had used the Basher before. They came up with this.

Big Job: *Install groupware and train team on it*   **Deadline:** *March 28*

Tracking Check when done:	Doable Task Specific steps to complete the job:	Deadline Task will be completed by:
☐	*Meet with MIS for coaching on installation, features, how to use.*	*3/4 at 9:30 a.m.*
☐	*Install groupware on my computer.*	*3/6*
☐	*Get coaching from Jean, who's already using it in her department.*	*3/10 at 3:30 p.m.*
☐	*Practice with tutorial.*	*3/17*
☐	*Schedule times to install on each team member's computer.*	*Week of 3/17*
☐	*Install software.*	*Week of 3/24*
☐	*Prepare training session for team.*	*3/25*
☐	*Conduct training session.*	*3/26*

With the Procrastination Basher, George was able to get a handle on all the facets of the job and begin tackling them—successfully—one at a time.

You Try It!

There's no time like the present to give the Procrastination Basher a try. Use it for a job you've been putting off for a while or one you're waiting until the last minute to complete, then break it down using the Procrastination Basher technique.

Big Job: _____ **Deadline:** _____

Tracking Check when done:	Doable Task Specific steps to complete the job:	Deadline Task will be completed by:
☐		
☐		
☐		
☐		
☐		
☐		

Some More Tips

- Ask an experienced internal partner or leader for ideas on how to break it down further.
- Double-check your deadlines to make sure they're realistic. (The last thing you want to do is set yourself up for failure as you try to switch to a productive habit.)
- If you're a tried-and-true procrastinator, ask someone to hold you accountable for implementing your plan.

Managing Yourself

There might be times when the Basher won't seem to be enough to help you quit procrastinating and get on with a job. That's when you need to use the second part of conquering procrastination—managing yourself.

Do you procrastinate because you are too busy? It sounds plausible, but that's not the real reason people procrastinate. Have you ever heard the phrase "If you want something done quickly, give it to a busy person"? The truth is that busy people are usually pretty good at accomplishing a lot. The five most common and real reasons for procrastination are shown below along with some tactics for addressing them.

Cause	Tactic for Addressing the Problem
Confusion ■ *"I don't know how to do this or where to start."* ■ *"I don't even know why I'm doing this."* ■ *"I got off to a good start, but now I'm not sure what to do next."*	■ Ask your leader or an experienced coworker for coaching on ways to approach the job. Get their help in filling out the Procrastination Basher. ■ Ask those who assigned you the work or who will use your work to describe why it's important, what outcome they expect, and how they'll use it. ■ Realize that the best-laid plans don't always work. The moment you start "going in circles," ask for help to identify steps for getting back on track.
Boredom ■ *"This job is mundane, routine."* ■ *"The job is so tedious."*	■ Try to look for the positive aspects of the job. Are any parts of it actually enjoyable? It's true that boring jobs aren't very challenging or risky, but is there a way you can enjoy the easiness of the job? ■ Plan a reward for yourself when you finish the job. ■ Make the mundane job top priority if possible. Take action to get it done sooner rather than later. Dreading it only makes you feel bad longer!

Cause	Tactic for Addressing the Problem
Anxiety ■ *"What if I can't do it well?"* ■ *"What if others don't like the way I'm approaching this?"* ■ *"The job is difficult."*	■ Ask your leader or an experienced team member for coaching on the level of quality needed. Maybe you think they expect more than they do. ■ Ask others to tell you if you're making the job more difficult than it needs to be and suggest ways to simplify it.
Frustration/Resentment ■ *"No one will notice or care."* ■ *"This seems like busywork. No one will use this."* ■ *"I can't get people to cooperate with me. . . . I'm hitting a brick wall."*	■ Check with the appropriate person(s) on whether it really should be done. ■ Identify who the work will help and how. ■ Ask your leader for coaching on how to overcome the barriers others seem to be creating. Or, if appropriate, ask your leader to step in and help you break down the barriers.
Tiredness ■ *"I don't have the energy to do this."*	■ Plan to work on the task at the time of day when you have the most energy. ■ Perhaps overcommitment is your problem, not procrastination. Ask your leader or a trusted team member for his or her perspective. ■ Maybe you think you must do the job better, more often, faster than it really needs to be done. Check with the person who assigned the job to make sure you understand what constitutes a "good job." ■ Take a few (but not too many!) short breaks as you're completing the job. ■ Don't assume that you have to do it all by yourself. Consider asking a team member or internal partner for help with one or more actions on your Basher.

Dear Madame Make It Happen,

What's the big deal about procrastination? I know that it sometimes makes things tough on me when a deadline gets close, but it really doesn't affect anyone's productivity but my own, and I work better under pressure.

Larry Laidback

Dear Larry,

It might be a little shortsighted to think that your procrastination affects only you. For example, procrastination can have these effects on others:

- *If you wait until the last minute to complete a task that you find requires the input or involvement of others, they might have to immediately drop what they're doing to help you. This interrupts the work they had planned, and they might not be able to contribute as well as they could have if they'd been given more time.*

- *It might take more than you thought to complete the task. As a result, you can't perform to the level of quality needed. Or, you produce quality work, but miss your deadline.*

In either of these cases, people begin to lose trust in your ability to meet commitments. And they might begin to feel that you're taking advantage of them.

Madame Make It Happen

You'll find further assistance on related subjects in the following sections: ***Being a Good Partner*** on page 64, ***Keeping Yourself Motivated in Tough Times*** on page 73, and ***Recognizing and Avoiding Perfectionism*** on page 79.

Link to . . .

Don't Slip Back

Dear Sam,

Good question! The answer is yes, and the right time is now. The tool is the Pitfall Planner.

Madame Make It Happen

Before You Begin to Slip

Slipping back into old behavior usually doesn't happen when things are going well. It happens when something breaks your routine and catches you off guard. Now—while you're enjoying the good feelings of being more productive and in control of your work life—is the time to plan your continued success.

This isn't negative thinking. Only the most naive people expect to be able to keep up a new good habit without any further effort. If that were so, people would never have to make New Year's resolutions or go on a diet more than once in their lifetimes.

To maintain your new level of productivity, use the Pitfall Planner to plan what to do when the going gets rough. The following example shows how the planner works.

- Column 1: List the new approach you'll use to increase your productivity.
- Column 2: List warning signs that could alert you to the fact that you might be slipping.
- Column 3: Write down what might make it hard to stick to your new behaviors.
- Column 4: Write the ways you can avoid slipping into old, less productive habits.

The Pitfall Planner

New, More Productive Approach	Warning Signals that I'm Slipping	What Might Cause a Slip	Strategies to Avoid a Slip
Keeping my work area clean and my files updated.	*Unorganized piles of things on my work surface.* *Lots of unopened mail.*	*Toward the end of the project, when everyone gets a little crazy.*	*Spend the last 10 minutes of the workday making sure everything is in its "home base."*
Setting boundaries to keep coworkers' interruptions at a minimum.	*I don't tell people when I'm too busy to talk.* *I give people the message that I like their pop-in visits.*	*When I'm not under the gun to meet a deadline.* *Friday afternoons.* *When I'm working on something that's difficult.*	*Make it a habit to ask people if we can talk at lunch or during a break. That way they'll learn that I'm serious about not being interrupted for small talk.*
Staying positive even when things get hectic.	*Tension headaches.* *People asking me if I'm OK.* *Noticing that my temper is just a little bit shorter.*	*When we get too many special orders and everyone is frantic.* *At the end of each quarter.*	*Remember that I'm in charge of how I react. Take a walk at lunch to get away from the tension.* *Take some deep breaths when I'm overwhelmed.*
Doing what I know I've got to do instead of procrastinating.	*Making one more excuse AGAIN for not beginning.* *Reading junk mail.* *Reorganizing things that are already organized.*	*Every time changes happen.* *When I just want to keep doing things the old way because that's what I'm comfortable with.*	*Remember to break the job into small tasks.* *Use the Procrastination Basher to keep track of my progress and to keep me on track.*

You Try It!

Using the sample as a guide, create your own list of ways to spot warning signals and avoid slipping back into unproductive behaviors.

New, More Productive Approach	Warning Signals that I'm Slipping	What Might Cause a Slip	Strategies to Avoid a Slip
_____	_____	_____	_____
_____	_____	_____	_____
_____	_____	_____	_____
_____	_____	_____	_____
_____	_____	_____	_____
_____	_____	_____	_____

I PREDICT REALLY SUCCESSFUL PEOPLE WILL ADD THINGS TO THIS LIST AS THEY THINK OF THEM.

Personal Productivity Group Discussion Guide

A great truth in life is that *you* have power to change the way you work to get the right things done, more effectively and more quickly. But the opposite of one great truth is often another great truth. *Others* also can have a big impact on your productivity. This section will help you and your coworkers and leaders help one another to be more productive.

How to Use This Group Discussion Guide

On the next several pages are discussion questions for each of the 18 topics in this book. The questions will help you and the people you work with to share and explore ideas about productivity. Before discussing any topic, participants should read the topic thoroughly. Here are some ways to use these discussion questions.

- The next time you hold a meeting where the agenda is not full, take 15–30 minutes to discuss the questions for one of the topics. Identify the top three ways that meeting participants will help one another be more productive relative to that topic.

- To continually enhance the performance of your department or team, schedule an hour every three months to discuss the questions for one or more topics. Use the first 15 minutes to evaluate how your group did on last quarter's topic(s). Make sure to identify specific actions your group will take to improve productivity.

- Ask each member of your department or team to volunteer to "champion" a topic. Have each person thoroughly review his or her topic and begin applying the tips and tactics to increase productivity. Regularly, have each department member take a turn leading a discussion on his or her topic. Have the member first share personal experiences, lessons learned, and tips, then follow that with a group discussion using the questions for the topic.

Examining Your Priorities

1. What are the most important tasks or objectives for our group to achieve?

2. What are the best ways for us to find out what's important?

3. Are we spending the appropriate amount of time on important/urgent and important/not urgent tasks?

What to Do When Everything Is Top Priority

4. What competing goals do we have?

5. Who can best help us prioritize competing goals?

6. What one tip can each of us share for effectively handling multiple priorities?

Staying on Track

7. What feedback have we gotten that shows whether we are on the right track?

8. Where can we get feedback on how appropriately we are spending our time?

9. How can we help one another recognize when we are—or aren't—on the right track?

10. How can we support one another so we can prioritize more quickly and accurately?

Organizing Your Work Area

11. How can we better organize the material, tools, or information we all share?

12. What are examples of organizing that have worked best for each of us?

13. What is the most disorganized area in our department, and how can we organize it?

Keeping Track of Your Time and Tasks

14. What are examples of scheduling practices that have worked well for each of us?

15. What are the biggest challenges to keeping track of our time and responsibilities? What ideas do we have to address those challenges?

Handling Interruptions

16. In our work environment, what are good ways to signal that we are too busy to talk?

17. What kinds of questions or tasks should we never consider to be an interruption?

18. What can we do to make sure we aren't interrupting?

Making Meetings Productive

19. Which disruptive meeting behavior occurs in our team? How can we help one another to avoid that behavior?

20. Which productive meeting practices will we put into place immediately?

Making a Basic Plan

21. Which of our tasks require advance planning—and the development of "Plan B"?

22. What are examples of contingency plans we have made?

Making the Best Use of Communication Tools

23. When is it best to use voice mail, e-mail, or a memo in our group? Outside our group?

24. What are our main frustrations with the e-mail or voice mail messages or memos we've received, and what would we like to see happen differently?

25. Which of our communication tools have generated positive feedback?

26. Under what circumstances do we expect to receive a personal visit or phone call rather than an e-mail or voice mail message or memo?

Networking

27. What kind of information is not available inside our group that would be important for us to know about? Who can we get that information from?

28. What has each of us done to effectively build a network?

Getting Support from Others

29. What kind of tasks or situations most often require us to help one another?

30. What can get in the way of asking for or getting help from a teammate?

31. What should we do if we don't think we can help someone who has asked for it?

Making Clear Agreements

32. What are examples of unclear agreements we have made with one another or with internal partners in the past? What were the causes? What were the results? What would we do differently next time?

33. What words/terms are often misunderstood across groups in our organization?

34. How can we clarify roles when working with one another or with internal partners?

35. What kinds of assumptions are we in danger of making about roles, rules, partners, etc., because of our group's perspective?

Being a Good Partner

36. What are the characteristics of a good partner? What are the characteristics of an ineffective partner?

37. What information can we share to aid our partners?

38. What would be a good way to address conflicts within our group or between members of our group and other groups?

39. What are our best opportunities to request and accept feedback?

Effective Follow-Up

40. What tasks or activities tend to fall through the cracks? What follow-up process can we put in place to make sure this doesn't happen?

41. What are the best ways to remind our coworkers of commitments without being a pest?

Keeping Yourself Motivated in Tough Times

42. What situations or work responsibilities make it tough for our team to stay motivated?

43. What negative attitudes are more common in our team, and how can we reframe them into more positive attitudes? (What's the "bright side" or "silver lining"?)

44. How can we acknowledge or reward ourselves for good work?

45. What can we change to avoid demotivating times?

Recognizing and Avoiding Perfectionism

46. Which tasks do we spend too much time on in order to achieve perfection?

47. How can we get a better understanding of the appropriate level of quality for our work?

Conquering Procrastination

48. What are the main reasons we procrastinate? What can we do to address those causes?

49. How does procrastination affect our own or one another's productivity?

Don't Slip Back

50. What are the top three most productive practices from this handbook that our group will implement?

51. What might indicate that we are not implementing these practices successfully? How will we know when we're successful?

52. What can we do to help one another use productive practices?

Other Books from DDI Press

The Service Leaders Club by William C. Byham, Ph.D., and Ray Crew, with James H.S. Davis.

The Selection Solution: Solving the Mystery of Matching People to Jobs by William C. Byham, Ph.D., with Steven M. Krauzer.

Team Leader's Survival Guide by Jeanne M. Wilson and Jill A. George, Ph.D.

Team Member's Survival Guide by Jill A. George, Ph.D., and Jeanne M. Wilson.

We'd Love to Hear from You!

Now that you've used some of our tips and tools for improving your productivity, we'd love to hear from you. Here are several ways to reach us:

Write to us at: Development Dimensions International

World Headquarters—Pittsburgh

Attention: Personal Productivity

1225 Washington Pike

Bridgeville, PA 15017-2838

Fax us at: 412-257-3916[*]

E-mail us at: ddidirect@ddiworld.com

For more information about our training and consulting services, please:

Call us at: Customer Information Center at 1-800-933-4463

between 8:00 a.m. and 5:30 p.m. (EST), Monday

through Friday.

Visit our web site: http://www.ddiworld.com

To place an order for additional copies of *Personal Productivity: Tips and Tools for Daily Success* or other books from DDI Press, please call 1-800-334-1514.

Thanks again for using *Personal Productivity: Tips and Tools for Daily Success.*

[*]As of April 30, 1998, the 412 area code will be replaced with 724.